Being Ethical

Other Books of Interest from St. Augustine's Press

James V. Schall, *On the Principles of Taxing Beer:*
And Other Brief Philosophical Essays

James V. Schall, *At a Breezy Time of Day*

Ralph McInerny, *The Defamation of Pius XII*

Ralph McInerny, *Good Knights: Eight Stories*

Ralph McInerny, *The Soul of Wit*

Ralph McInerny, *Let's Read Latin*

Marvin R. O'Connell, *Telling Stories that Matter: Memoirs and Essays*

Rémi Brague, *Moderately Modern*

Christopher Kaczor, *O Rare Ralph McInerny*

Josef Pieper, *A Journey to Point Omega: Autobiography from 1964*

Peter Kreeft, *Socrates' Children: The 100 Greatest Philosophers*

Peter Kreeft, *Ethics for Beginners: 52 "Big Ideas" from 32 Great Minds*

John von Heyking, *Comprehensive Judgment and Absolute Selflessness:*
Winston Churchill on Politics as Friendship

Joseph Bottum, *The Decline of the Novel*

Roger Scruton, *An Intelligent Person's Guide to Modern Culture*

Roger Scruton, *The Meaning of Conservatism: Revised 3rd Edition*

Roger Scruton, *The Politics of Culture and Other Essays*

Roger Scruton, *On Hunting*

Leon J. Podles, *Losing the Good Portion:*
Why Men Are Alienated from Christianity

Allen Mendenhall, *Shouting Softly: Lines on Law, Literature, and Culture*

René Girard, *A Theater of Envy: William Shakespeare*

Frederic Raphael and Joseph Epstein, *Where Were We?:*
The Conversation Continues

C. S. Lewis and Don Giovanni Calabria, *The Latin Letters of C. S. Lewis*

Being Ethical
D. Q. McInerny

ST. AUGUSTINE'S PRESS
South Bend, Indiana

Copyright © 2020 by D. Q. McInerny

All rights reserved. No part of this book may be reproduced, stored in a retrieval system, or transmitted, in any form or by any means, electronic, mechanical, photocopying, recording, or otherwise, without the prior permission of St. Augustine's Press.

Manufactured in the United States of America.

1 2 3 4ʹ5 6   26 25 24 23 22 21 20

Library of Congress Cataloging-in-Publication Data

Names: McInerny, Dennis Q.; author.
Title: Being ethical / D. Q. McInerny.
Identifiers: LCCN 2020034308 (print)
LCCN 2020034309 (ebook) | ISBN
9781587310683 (hardcover)
ISBN 9781587310690 (paperback)
ISBN 9781587310706 (ebook)
Subjects: LCSH: Ethics.
Classification: LCC BJ1012 .M417 2020 (print)
LCC BJ1012 (ebook)
DDC 170--dc23
LC record available at https://lccn.loc.gov/2020034308
LC ebook record available at https://lccn.loc.gov/2020034309

∞ The paper used in this publication meets the minimum requirements of the American National Standard for Information Sciences – Permanence of Paper for Printed Materials, ANSI Z39.48-1984.

St. Augustine's Press
www.staugustine.net

Table of Contents

Foreword

Two of the most important judgments we make over the course of our lives have to do with the distinction between good and evil. Those judgments shape the moral contours of our lives, reveal what kind of people we choose to be. Ethics, the subject of this book, is the science of the good and the bad, specifically, of the moral good and bad. We call all sorts of things good or bad which either have nothing to do with morality, or relate to it only tangentially. We identify something as morally good or bad when it has a direct bearing on human action, in all its forms—what we think, what we say, what we do. In ethics our principal focus is on the good, simply to give proper deference to reality. The good is more basic than the bad. The bad exists parasitically in relation to the good; if there were no good, there could be no evil.

What is the good? At a basic level, the level at which ethics begins, it is simply whatever elicits a positive response from us. The good is what pleases us, ignites desire; it is something we want to get close to and, if possible, to possess. The overall effect the good has on us is best expressed by a single word—love. In sum, the good is what we love, what we desire, what we want to have.

Right and wrong are the common terms by which we describe our behavior as it relates to good and evil. We act rightly to the extent that our behavior is directed toward the achievement of the good, wrongly, if our behavior is such so as to thwart our achieving the good. The fundamental principles that govern the science of ethics are rather simple and straightforward, as you will see as you delve into the pages that follow. Moreover, many of them will already be quite familiar to you, because all of us have, by nature, something like an instinctive knowledge of the elementary ethical principles.

Ethics, as a science, has been around for a long time, and as is the case with several other sciences, in this one too we owe much to the ancient

Greeks for the foundational ideas and theories they have handed down to us. It is not surprising that the kind of thought with which ethics is concerned has a venerable history behind it, for since time immemorial we human beings have been preoccupied with questions regarding good and evil, regarding the right and wrong of human behavior, regarding the standards according to which human behavior is evaluated, regarding everything having to do with the moral realm.

Every society has its store of burning moral issues that it worries over and vigorously debates, and our society is no different in that respect. Disagreements abound regarding a variety of critically important questions: When does human life begin? What is a human person? Is abortion a more or less innocuous "choice," or is it tantamount to murder? Is the death penalty immoral? Should euthanasia be actively promoted? Should doctors assist people in committing suicide? What is the nature of marriage? Should economic issues take precedence over all others in determining the shape and direction of any political community? Should there be any limitations to free speech? Does the pervasive depiction of violence in the media have a deleterious effect on the children and youth of the country? Is human cloning, if possible, either desirable or permissible? Is there such a thing as an unjust war? To what extent is it right for any given nation state to interfere in the internal affairs of another nation state? Does the public sponsorship of gambling contribute to the corruption of the citizenry?

These and countless other issues of like kind are the business of ethics to deal with, for they all, to one degree or another, are moral issues, having to do with the right and the wrong of human behavior. Difficult moral questions such as those listed above admit of resolution only to the extent that they are dealt with rationally, and they can be dealt with rationally only to the extent that there are certain basic standards or criteria—the fundamental principles on which ethics is founded—according to which any particular issue can be analyzed and discussed. If people are not well versed in the fundamental principles on which ethics is founded, they are without the necessary wherewithal to solve the variety of pressing ethical problems that beset us today.

There are numberless excellent books on ethics which take as their purpose the close and detailed examination of one or several important ethical questions of the day, often presenting the opposing sides of a given question. This is the case study approach to ethics, and it is unquestionably very valuable. The book you have in your hands is not of that kind. This is a book on fundamentals. My purpose here is to lay out as clearly and cogently as I can, avoiding the use of technical language, the basic principles on which the science of ethics is founded, thereby making available to the reader the kind of knowledge which one must necessarily have in order to be able to handle ethical issues, be they routine or more than usually gnarled, in a confident and competent manner.

A word needs to be said as to what should be, but seldom is, an important consideration regarding the successful resolution of any difficult ethical question. It most certainly involves knowledge; one must be conversant with the fundamental principles of ethics. But more than knowledge is required. Being ethical is not simply a state of mind, it is a state of being, a way of living one's life that reflects the fundamental principles of ethics. An ethical person is one who not only thinks in a certain way, but who lives in a certain way, in whom there is a happy marriage between thought and action, between theory and practice. In the final analysis, then, so I believe, it is the ethical person who would be the most adept at dealing successfully with the full range of ethical questions.

One

Ethics Is about Human Behavior

To say that ethics is about human behavior is informative, but only up to a point, for so too are several other disciplines one could quickly name— history, sociology, psychology, anthropology, economics, political science. How does ethics differ from them? Each of those disciplines, without deviating from its central scientific commitment, could settle for a purely descriptive account of human nature. Ethics, like other sciences having to do with human behavior, is importantly concerned with description. That is where it begins. But then it goes on to take three further steps which are peculiar to its own scientific commitment: (1) it endeavors to explain human behavior, specially in terms of the causes of that behavior; (2) it evaluates human behavior; (3) it boldly prescribes for it. These three functions are optional for other human sciences, but not for ethics, and it executes each of them in ways that are uniquely its own.

Other sciences which deal with human behavior do at times evaluate that behavior, but they do so according to the strictly limited criteria dictated by those sciences. The economist evaluates behavior in economic terms—is it conducive to the increase or to the diminishment of wealth?—and the psychologist evaluates behavior in terms of whether or not it contributes to or detracts from sound mental health. Both the economist and the psychologist may talk about "good" and "bad" human behavior, but here the reference is to specifically economic or psychological goodness and badness. Sciences other than ethics may also provide explanations for human behavior, and they will at times even prescribe for it as well, but, once again, here the explanations and prescriptions will be made in terms of the limited concerns of the science in question. The economist tells us how to behave if we want to secure the material goods necessary to sustain a decent standard of living; the psychologist, for his part, provides directives which will, if followed, make for a condition marked by mental and emotional balance.

Ethics differs from all the other sciences that deal with human behavior by reason of the comprehensive view it takes of human nature itself. In describing human behavior, its principal concern is to identify just what it is, in that behavior, which makes it peculiarly *human,* what is it that is not just common to, but essential to, all human beings just as such? Ethics is not particularly interested in this or that particular type of behavior—say, political, or musical, or athletic—but focuses on the common denominators of human action which are to be found alike in the politician, in the musician, and in the athlete.

As students of ethics, we seek the most general explanations for human behavior we can find. To say that Jones did what he did because he wanted to bring about an appreciable increase in his income is interesting information as far as it goes, but we want to move beyond these specialized explanations and inquire into why Jones, or any other human being, does anything at all. What moves us to act, *as human beings*, whatever the specific nature of an action?

Ethical evaluation is *moral* evaluation. To evaluate an act from a moral point of view is to identify it as either a good or a bad act, simply in terms of its being a human act, that is, an act performed by a rational agent who is the conscious, originating source of his own actions. To be good or bad morally is to be good or bad as a person, to either succeed or fail on the foundational level of the simply human. It is quite possible, and sometimes common, for someone to be good, even excellent, in a certain type of behavior—let us say, athletic or musical—but who is not particularly impressive just as a human being. Smith is an Olympic gold medalist and plays the harmonica with the verve of a veritable virtuoso, but you would be reluctant to introduce him to your kid sister.

Ethics is boldly, persistently, unabashedly prescriptive. It is very much in the business of telling us how we should live our lives. But once again, in this case, the emphasis is on the human just as human. Ethics has no direct interest in telling us how to be good musicians, or athletes, or scientists. Its purpose is to give us guidelines which will help us to be good human beings, which, as far as ethics is concerned, is the most important way of being good. Do we really consider it to be a desirable state of affairs—ethics asks of us—to be someone who is, say, the most learned and competent logician the world has ever known, and yet be a complete cad as a person?

To sum up. Ethics is a science which treats of human behavior by describing it, explaining it, evaluating it, and prescribing for it. It is concerned with human behavior precisely as human, that is, as reflecting the nature which is common to all of us as rational creatures.

Two

Human Behavior Precisely as Human

What is human behavior? What is its most prominent, its most character-istic, its defining feature? It is this: all human behavior is oriented toward, is motivated by, purpose.

Human beings are preeminently purposeful creatures. We are naturally goal-oriented; our actions are expressly calculated to get us to a specific somewhere, to achieve a definite something. In fact, what we identify as an action is defined by the end, the purpose, toward which it is directed. If there is no discernible purpose, there is no identifiable action. The purpose of an action is almost always explicitly stated in the very description of the action itself. Baking a cake, writing a letter, buying a book: the purpose of the baking is the cake; of the writing, the letter; of the buying, a book. We walk to get to the drug store, or to Aunt Polly's place. But don't we, you might ask, at times just walk, with no particular purpose in mind? It would be hard to imagine such a case. We may not be walking to arrive at a par-ticular location, but there is always some purpose behind that activity: we walk to get exercise, to settle a Thanksgiving dinner, to alleviate nervousness, to get out of the house and away from the in-laws, to work out a plot for a short story, or simply to glean the simple pleasures which accompany walk-ing itself. No genuinely human action is without purpose.

But the fact that we are purposeful creatures scarcely makes us unique in that respect. Truth to tell, we are residents of a universe that is fairly awash in purpose. Animals, from the simplest to the most complex, act purposefully. Consider the measured, sly movements of the red fox as he stalks an unsuspecting squad of yellow and brown ducklings dutifully trail-ing behind their mallard mother. That fox is up to something very definite: the possibility of securing a succulent duckling dinner. Plants act purpose-fully as well, in the way they drive their roots deep into the soil for stability and sustenance, and in the ingenious manner they adjust the plane of their leaves to get maximum exposure to the sun. Purposeful activity is even found on the level of inorganic being, everywhere you look. The chemical elements do not behave haphazardly in the way they interact with one another; if they did, there would be no science of chemistry. It's rather ingenius when you think about it, how hydrogen and oxygen get together in a wonderfully regular way to give us something entirely new—water.

To claim that all things act purposefully does not mean that all things are conscious of the purposes for which they act. It simply means that their actions are end-oriented, that they invariably terminate in a definite and predictable way. It is predictability that makes possible the practical applications of science. When the chemist combines hydrogen and oxygen in the right amounts and proportions and adds a fillip of electricity to the mix, he does not have to guess at the outcome. The end is pre-ordained, for such is the determinism that makes nature nature.

What is the cosmic upshot of the great drama of purposefulness in which all of us are involved? In a word, it is order. We can thank the fact that all things always or for the most part act for the sake of an end that we live in an ordered universe. This order brings with it any number of priceless benefits, not the least of which is that it allows for the possibility of life.

If purpose is to be found everywhere we look, how does it add anything special to human behavior? How are we different from the foxes, the foxgloves, and the hydrogen and oxygen? Let's start with the hydrogen and oxygen. While these two gases can accommodatingly behave in ways that arrive at a precisely predictable end, we would be hesitant to say that, in doing so, they know what they are doing. Their purposeful behavior is quite unconscious. And so too with the activities of plant life. Things are quite different, however, once we enter the animal kingdom. It would be interesting to know what is going on in the head of that fox as he stalks those hapless ducklings. He is surely conscious. But is he engaged in an activity that bears some analogy to human thinking? The only way we could find out is to ask the fox, and, so far at any rate, the fox is not talking.

Because we have no access to the peculiar kind of consciousness enjoyed by animals, we cannot be sure just how their consciousness relates to their purposeful activity. But it seems reasonable to infer from their behavior that, while they clearly act consciously for the sake of achieving specific ends, it is not at all evident that they are conscious of those ends precisely as ends. In other words, they do not consciously set them up as goals for action, by first deliberating over them, and then making a choice regarding the most effective action to take in order to reach those goals. A simpler way of putting the matter is to say that animals act purposefully under the guiding impetus of instinct, the efficiency of which can be quite amazing.

Be those things as they may, what we can say with complete confidence—because here we have direct, incontrovertible evidence on our side—is that what signally distinguishes human behavior is that, not only do we consciously act for the sake of achieving specific ends, we are conscious of the fact that we are doing precisely that. We know the "why" behind our actions. We are purposeful creatures, and we are aware of ourselves as purposeful creatures. The proof of our being conscious of purpose just as purpose, is to be found in the fact that we can pick our purposes. When it comes down to the choice of particular goods, we are not determined to any one of them to the exclusion of the others. In the most general way, we always choose what we deem will be good for us, but what particular form the good will take for us, here and now, in this situation, that is up to us to decide. Barbara has been proposed to by both Brian and Bruce, each of whom, as judged by an array of reliable standards, is an unquestionably good guy, a clear candidate for being Mr. Right. To whom will she say Yes? The answer to the question is not predetermined by the stars, by Barbara's sociological circumstances, nor by her DNA. The choice is hers, as the unique individual who is Barbara.

So, human behavior is specifically characterized by the fact that we consciously act for the sake of an end, and we know we are doing that. To act in such a way is to act rationally. The beauty and benefit of rational activity is that we can see where it is headed, the purpose toward which it is directed. Irrational activity, on the other hand, is best described as activity in which we can divine no purpose. It appears to us as random and directionless, motion without meaning.

We next have to consider what is added to human behavior by calling it ethical.

Three

What Is Ethical Behavior?

On occasion, and usually by way of making a definite compliment, we will refer to certain people as "ethical." If negative considerations prevail, we will call certain other people "unethical." What are we attempting to communicate by applying these designations to our fellows?

The essence of human behavior, we now know, lies in the fact that it is consciously and deliberately directed toward the achievement of specific ends. It is purposeful behavior, and this is just another way of saying that it is rational behavior. Purposeful behavior can be successful or unsuccessful, its success being dependent on its achieving the end toward which it is directed. When the end of a particular act is achieved, it is potentially perfective of the agent responsible for the act. This means that, if it is the right kind of end, its achievement will improve the condition of the agent in one way or another. Allison reaches for the ripe, red apple dangling seductively over her head. She carefully disengages it from its branch, bites into it, and in short order has reduced it to its core. It was a very good apple, and Allison, for having eaten it, is now better off, at one level of her being, than she was before.

Some actions, like picking an apple off a tree, are so undemanding that one can get them right the first time. Others require much practice. A professional field goal kicker, with years of experience behind him, seldom fails to put the football between the uprights. He invariably achieves the end of the highly specialized, and highly paid, act for which he is principally known to his lustily cheering fans.

We have already taken note of the fact that a person can be very adept at performing certain specialized types of actions—say, as an athlete, or musician, or artist—and yet be considerably less than illustrious just as a person. This is a problematic situation. To fall short on the elementary human level, to be incompetent as a person, is something that cannot be compensated for, neutralized, or rendered nugatory by even the most spec-tacular performances in activities which are not explicitly moral in character. To fail as a person is to fail in the only way that really counts, and no amount of other successes can make up for it.

An ethical person is one who has his priorities straight, in the critical sense that he knows that the most important way to be perfected is morally, which is to say, precisely as a human person. The unethical person, for what-ever reason, is without this knowledge, or he may have the knowledge but he lacks the willpower to act on it.

Ethical human behavior is truly human behavior, for it is characteristic of those who put a premium on always acting in ways that are constructive of their humanity, that reflect their essential nature as rational agents, agents who act for the sake of ends that are perfective of them *as persons*. An ethical person is one who is successful in achieving the right kind of ends, what we might describe simply as humanizing ends.

We need to come to better terms with the particulars of those kinds of ends. But first we have to tend to some additional basic groundwork, by looking more closely at the idea of end itself, surely one of the key ideas in ethics.

Four

The Idea of End

There is nothing particularly challenging, from a conceptual point of view, about the idea of end. An end is simply "that for the sake of which" any act is done, and as such it is, as we saw, defining of the act itself. Every act, if it is a bona fide act, has a purpose built right into it; indeed, it is purpose that makes an act an act. Aristotle regularly reminds us that every agent acts for the sake of an end; that is what being an agent is all about. As agents, we do whatever we do for the sake of achieving particular ends, and all ends, if they have any goodness whatever to them, will be perfective of us in one way or another, either importantly or not so importantly. When we act specifically as moral agents, we do whatever we do to achieve ends which will be perfective of us morally, that is, precisely as persons. Now, we are all by nature moral agents, but that does not mean that we are by nature the most efficient of moral agents. We all too frequently flub up when it comes to successfully achieving moral ends.

It is the end that we seek to achieve by our actions which motivates us, which spurs us to action. The whole process begins in the mind, in the form of an idea, a conceptual representation of the end we want to achieve, the purpose we want to realize. Thus, we say that the end is first in conception, last in execution. Before the expert kicker can kick a field goal he must first have it in mind to do just that. He forms the intention to kick a field goal. Thought precedes action, and the quality and clarity of the thought will have a direct bearing on the success of the action it is intended to instigate.

But what is it about any end which we have in mind that prompts us to take the requisite action to achieve it? In what lies its attractiveness for us? The answer to those questions leads us back to the foundational nature of the good. Each and every end that we seek to achieve—no exceptions allowed here—we seek to achieve because we perceive it as good. And the good, by definition, is what we desire and, in one way or another, want to take possession of. The reason Allison picked the apple off that tree was because she saw it as a good, hence, as something desirable. The good we are talking about here is not an abstraction. It is a concrete reality, embodied in a specific object, such as Allison's apple, or, for that matter, Allison herself, for, as it happens, she is the apple of Arthur's eye.

All right, fine: we pursue any particular end because we see it as a good. But why do we see it as good? In what does the goodness of the end consist, as far as we are concerned? It consists in the fact that we interpret its possession as perfective of us, as somehow or other capable of improving our condition, enhancing our general state of being. To be sure, the nature of the "perfection" brought about in the agent as the result of achieving a particular end might be of a very humble sort, such as the somatic satisfaction Allison felt after eating the apple.

It is important that we take special note of the very significant fusion that takes place in our minds preliminary to performing any particular act—a fusion between the idea of end and the idea of the good. The two ideas become effectively one and the same. What we seek as an end we seek as a good. It is the idea of the good, the desire for the good, which provides the foundational intelligibility for all of our actions. We can confidently make the grand claim that it is the good, what we perceive to be good, which accounts for everything we do. The good rules our lives.

Ends inevitably entail means. To commit oneself to a particular end is, at least implicitly, to commit oneself to the means which are required to achieve that end. We cannot be serious in the attention we are directing toward any end, cannot really mean it when we tell ourselves that we regard it as a good, if we are not willing to do whatever it takes in order to possess it. The difficulty involved in achieving different ends can of course vary enormously; it all depends on the nature of the end in question. There is much less involved in picking an apple off a tree than in picking a husband.

We pursue ends because we see them as good; we see them as good because we interpret them as somehow beneficial to us. This does not mean that being ethical amounts to no more than assuaging our egos, as if it were essentially a matter of subjective gratification. To be sure, we always act as subjects, but we should not act "subjectively" in a negative sense, that is, out of narrow-minded selfishness. Ideally, we act as subjects who make judgments according to criteria that are founded in the objective order of things.

Five

Standards

We need to pause at this point and give some systematic consideration to the matter of evaluation, which plays an important role in ethics. As moral agents, all of us, willy nilly, are evaluators, judges. We are continuously having to make judgments regarding the moral worth of our actions, assessing the quality of our behavior

When we evaluate something, anything at all, we are estimating its worth according to certain standards. A closer analysis of the evaluating process reveals that it embodies three distinct elements: there is the one who is doing the evaluating, the object being evaluated, and the standards according to which the evaluation is made. If an evaluation is itself to have any value, those doing the evaluating must be qualified for the job, meaning that they must be familiar with (a) the objects being evaluated and (b) the standards by which they are evaluated. The results of evaluations are expressed in quantitative or qualitative terms. Examples of quantitative evaluation: "a ten"; "86.7%"; "in the top one-third of the class." Examples of qualitative evaluation: "excellent"; "rather good"; "so-so."

The evaluations we make in ethics are always qualitative. Is this a disadvantage? It would seem, at first blush, that quantitative evaluations are more accurate than qualitative ones, but this can be deceptive. When a judge for an Olympic competition assigns a "ten" to a particular performance, can that be considered more precise, more informative, than describing the performance as "flawless" or "perfect"? If another judge assigned a "9.2" to the same performance, was that judge being more or less precise than the one who wrote down "10"?

If an evaluation is not made according to recognized standards, it becomes no more than the expression of the purely personal opinion of the evaluator, and is thus of only biographical interest. The standards by which we evaluate can vary greatly. Some standards, like the rules of baseball, can be quite detailed and are laid down in clear, explicit terms. It is by following these rules that an umpire judges whether a pitch is a ball or a strike, or whether a runner sliding into second base is safe or out. Certain things are permitted in baseball, and certain things are prohibited, according to the rules of the game. Those rules, the standards according to which the game is to be played, not only give structure and coherence to the game, they actually bring it into existence as the peculiar kind of organized athletic activity it is, to which we assign the term "game." Without the rules governing the actions of the players, there would be no game, nothing but haphazard movement, with no particular rhyme or reason to it. The unfortunate spectator would be utterly confused, and to allay his frustration could be driven to gorge himself on peanuts and Crackerjacks, not to mention beer. In some respects, life itself is not radically unlike the game of baseball, for all of us must adhere to certain standards that govern our behavior, otherwise interpersonal relations would be anarchic, and life, although not now always beautiful, would then be positively ugly.

Seldom do we find ourselves, on any given day, always explicitly aware of the full range of standards that frame the ethical life, and which serve as the practical guidelines for our behavior, any more than the professional baseball player has continual explicit awareness of the rules of baseball, although he surely knows them, through assimilation. His knowledge of the rules is displayed in how he actually behaves, by the way he conducts himself on the field. It is the same with us regarding the basic rules of morality. They are deeply imbedded in our common consciousness as moral agents. If one or another of these rules were to be given explicit expression in our presence, we would doubtless promptly recognize it as something with which we are already quite familiar. "We should do no willful harm to anyone." Yes, of course, we reply. "Do unto others as you would have them do unto you." Beautiful! I believe it, we say. "Always tell the truth." Exactly, we concur, and everyone should abide by that honorable dictum, especially Uncle Frank.

As a tentative, and not fully adequate, description of the meaning of "being ethical," we could say that it consists in living in such a way that one's behavior is regularly being governed and guided by stock ethical standards. That is certainly an important part of the picture, as observed from the outside as it were, but the description is not fully adequate because being ethical can never be a matter of simply following the rules. It is *how* we follow the rules that spells the difference. To follow an ethical rule mechanically, as one who does not see the intrinsic worth of the rule, understood as a dictate of reason, is to function, not as a responsible moral agent, but as an automaton. If something is in fact a sound ethical standard, such as the principle which tells us that we should always be truthful, then allowing it to be a fixed shaping influence on one's behavior is an eminently rational thing to do, for to live according to such a principle is simply to live humanly, to fulfill oneself as a human being, a rational creature.

A sound ethical standard has an inherent rightness to it, and that is why it makes a direct appeal to human reason. It is not an arbitrary mandate, a rule which is to be obeyed simply because "that's the way it is," or because you might fear the penalties you could be subject to if you do not obey it. Consider the Golden Rule: "Do unto others as you would have others do unto you." It would be a crude misconstruing of the rule to interpret it as advocating a kind of tit-for-tat morality: I'll scratch your back if you scratch mine, or, negatively, I won't scratch your face if you don't scratch mine. With that kind of interpretation, all "ethical" behavior would amount to little more than an exercise in concentrated, albeit camouflaged, egotism, where the principal preoccupation of each person becomes looking after Number One.

The beauty and poignancy of the Golden Rule lies in the fact that it calls for a recognition, on the part of all parties concerned (i.e., all of us), of the inestimable worth of each human person. It then specifies the behavior that logically and inevitably should follow upon that recognition. The mutuality of beneficent behavior, one to another, is founded on the fact that each person sees the intrinsic worth of the other person. I act beneficently toward the other, not principally because I expect beneficent behavior in return, but because I recognize that the other is a person and, just as a person, is deserving of such behavior. However, given the pervasiveness of the ideal, I can reasonably expect that I will in fact receive beneficent behavior in return, and that is because the other person also sees me as a person, and responds accordingly.

Six

Ends Are Many and Varied

We do whatever we do for the sake of an end—a wonderfully rational way in which to behave! It is the end that gives meaning to every action we perform, and that contributes to the meaning of our life as a whole. Over the course of a given day we are pursuing any number of particular ends, and that is because, unless we have chosen to become vegetating couch potatoes, an average day for us is fairly jam-packed with particular acts, most of which are of no great consequence. Where there is an act, there is an end. The ends we pursue over the course of an entire lifetime are beyond counting; they, and the acts to which they are conjoined, make up the very stuff of our lives, a life which can be described, at least from this perspective, as the sum total of the acts we perform from birth to death.

Many are the ends which we pursue. Quite so. But clearly we do not regard all those many and variegated ends as being on the same level, in terms of their intrinsic worth; some we take to be more important, sometimes considerably more important, than others. Because we regard all ends as goods—we would not pursue them if we did not see them as such—the choice of the specific acts we engage in is determined by how we rank the goods those acts are intended to achieve. Between two goods, P and Q, if I value P higher than Q, I will be inclined to take the action that will get me to P, rather than the action that will put Q in my possession. A nap is a good, and so is fish and chips, bird-watching, reading a novel, a conversation with a friend, visiting Paris, getting married, watching a tennis match, playing golf, gardening, and listening to a Mozart piano concerto. Probably no two of us would come up with an identical ranking for that list of goods, for none of us would be likely to give exactly the same value to each of them.

If we could imagine ourselves standing on a privileged promontory which would allow us to view all of the ends that are pursued over the course of a lifetime, we would see a huge complicated structure made up of a myriad of interrelated acts. With our binoculars we focus on two particular acts, A and B (with their accompanying ends), and note that they are related to one another in such a way that Act B is dependent on Act A, because Act B cannot be performed unless Act A is performed first. Herb cannot fly to Paris unless he first purchases the airline ticket. Most of our acts are related to one another in that way. I have a certain end in mind which I want to achieve, but the trail to the achievement of that end leads through the achievement of a number of preliminary ends. I want to achieve D. In order to do so I must first achieve A, B, and C. Although we have a great deal of freedom in the ends we pursue, there is a preestablished order in the way certain ends are related to others, and we have no choice but to submit to that order. I cannot arbitrarily leap over preliminary ends in order to achieve ends that are dependent on them.

If Susan wants to achieve a significant end like earning a medical degree, there is a whole raft of preliminary ends she must tend to, and in proper order. There are no shortcuts to the achievement of what Aristotle calls final ends—the major accomplishments of our lives. Limiting ourselves to the academic sphere, we know that before Susan can get an M.D., she has to earn a bachelor's degree, preferably in the sciences, which she could not even begin doing without a high school diploma in her possession, and there were any number of necessary steps she had to take preliminary to getting that diploma. I suppose, in order to get a complete picture, we would have to start with Susan graduating from pre-school, and in tracing her entire academic career we would discover a whole slew of particular ends that she would have to achieve—e.g., passing a course in organic chemistry in her junior year of college—before she finally reaches the final end which is the *Medicinae Doctor*, the Doctor of Medicine degree.

Given the way ends lead on to ends, there is a continual transmutation, over the course of time, of ends into means. For a significant period of her life, a B.S. in biology is the principal end toward the achievement of which Susan must dedicate herself, and achieving it will give shape and direction, in one way or another, to almost all of her actions, what with the peculiar demands of that end. Should she succeed in earning that degree, it then becomes a means by which the end of earning an M.D. is achieved. And so it goes. A reminder of a point made earlier, an obvious one: Ends cannot be separated from the means that have to be taken in order to reach them, so if Susan, when she matriculates to Colossal College, is more interested in partying than in studying, then one can doubt the earnestness of her declaration that she wants to be a doctor some day. To want the end is to want the means.

Another obvious point: an end must be realistically achievable, in terms of the actual capacities of the person who identifies it as a desirable good. We all applaud and admire the gumption and perseverance displayed by The Little Engine That Could, and we would consider its attitude worthy of emulation. However, in order to achieve any end, while we of course must be willing, we must also be able. It is one thing to identify an end as a good—and it is a necessary thing, for, once again, it is the perception of something as a good that moves us toward it—but we must match our desires with a realistic appraisal of our abilities to achieve what we desire. There are two pertinent meanings that can be attached to "desirable": (a) what should be desired because obtaining it will in fact be good for the desiring person; (b) what should be desired because it is possible for the desiring person actually to obtain it. Both invite serious consideration before we act.

In some situations there is almost a one-to-one correspondence between a particular end and the means required to achieve it. If Donny wants to lose weight, the first order of business for him would be to reduce his intake of calories. Donny may have his choice of diets, but dieting itself is the primary means he must adopt if he wants one day to gaze down smilingly at lower numbers on the bathroom scale. He must pay strict attention to the quantity and quality of what he eats. In this kind of situation there is no need to spend a lot of time mulling over means. They are clearly marked out for us, at least in their general contours.

If all roads lead to Rome, then we have many ways by which we can get there. The major ends we set out to achieve in our lives often offer a choice of means. Here is where we have to pause and do some serious deliberating, for although two roads might infallibly get us to Rome, we might discover, in examining them closely, that one is definitely better than the other, will get us to our destination more quickly, more safely, with less all-around trouble. We can waste much valuable time and energy in pursuing an end which is both worthy and possible by employing means which are a poor match for it because of their inefficiency. And it is possible for us to make so bad a choice of means that we never succeed in reaching an intended end, an end which could have been reached had we chosen means more suitable to it.

Rome has an accommodating permanency to it. If we don't get there this year, well, we can go next year, or the year after. But there is a determined time span within which certain ends must be pursued, otherwise they are inaccessible. They offer but a narrow window of opportunity, and we have to plan carefully and proceed promptly. If I want to see the cherry trees blossoming in Washington, D.C., my schedule will have to accord with that of the cherry trees. I can't put off my sightseeing trip until midsummer.

We need then to adopt means that are best ordered toward the end which we seek to achieve. Clear enough. We might call such means "efficient." They will get the job done, gain the end we have in mind. But should we always consider the best means to be the easiest means? I am going to offer an unorthodox opinion on that matter: No, the easiest means are not in each and every circumstance necessarily the best means. Sometimes there is merit in doing things the hard way, and that is because of the educational value to taking that way. Following the circuitous, perhaps even tortuous, route can teach us things that we otherwise would never learn, things that we would be better for knowing. This all makes sense, mind you, only if the end we seek to achieve is actually achieved.

Seven
Desire

Dogs doubtless desire, and so too, we can reasonably suppose, do cats, rats, and blue jays. But there is something absolutely unique about human desire, for its persistence, its pervasiveness, its inexhaustible potency. It has a depth to it not to be fathomed, a width not to be spanned. Desire will not leave us alone, and can at times be positively pestering in its tenacity. When that happens, when desire takes on almost a burdensome aspect, we might delude ourselves into thinking that we could do without desire, thank you. Vain thought. A life without desire would be unimaginably dull. Actually, it wouldn't be a life at all, for life is made up of action, and without desire there would be no action. Desire is the fire that ignites action. Absent desire, we would be as inert as stones, and, *pace* all geologists, as interesting.

The ends we zero in on and purposefully pursue are in the first instance always *our* goods, and that is because we have convinced ourselves, albeit perhaps at a very primitive level of consciousness, that the ends/goods, once possessed, are going to be, in some manner or another, beneficial to us. What takes place at this stage—where we initially react to a perceived good—is a dominantly emotional experience. And the emotion principally in play, positioned front and center, is love. The objects of our affection are just those things we identify as goods.

Now, you cannot have love without desire. It is a package deal. To love an object, really love it, means that you hanker after some kind of union with the object, and therefore you are inevitably moved toward it. Again, it is the emotion of desire that does the moving. That is why desire can make us so restless. It is constantly urging us on toward loved objects, things that catch our amorous eye and stir up thoughts of marriage, if only a marriage of convenience.

Desirable objects are simply loved objects, things we identify as goods, and therefore they are as many and varied as the ends/goods the pursuit of which determines the very structures of our lives. There is something especially serious, because always consequential, about genuinely desiring something, for desire is *the* motivating emotion. (Incidentally, all emotions motivate, in their differing ways. "Emotion" comes from the Latin *movere*, which means "to move.") Desire impels us toward the loved object. Should our response to a presumably loved object be an disinterested, "Well, that's nice," or, "Now, isn't that interesting," with no movement toward the object, then we can be sure there is no real desire involved, and, accordingly, neither is the presumed love real. We only act on what we really love, and so, just as real willing is to be distinguished from mere wishing, real loving is to be distinguished from mere liking. Tucked into every "I love that" is "I want that."

The nature of the emotion of desire, the passional expression of our pressing wants, is such that, once the object of our desire is actually attained, the desire cooperatively dissipates, wafts away on the morning breeze. Wally wants a raise, a bit of praise from Uncle Clayt, and to marry a gal just like the gal that married dear old dad. And, over time—Wally was a man on whom fortune tended to smile—all of these desires are fulfilled. The fulfillment of our desires has a quieting effect on us, we experience a pacifying contentment. It is a delectable state to be in, but unfortunately it is never a permanent one. Wally, for a while at least, is quiescently satisfied with his lot in life as the result of those three wants of his having been met.

But the drama is ongoing. When we get what we want, we are rarely completely content with it. Our satisfaction, though genuine, admits of qualifications; it may fill us up, but never to the very brim. And the initial intensity the satisfaction may have had eventually diminishes. There always seems to be, in retrospect, a disconcerting discrepancy between the loved object, as envisioned by us before it is actually possessed, and that same object once it is actually in our possession. Real disappointment, in one degree or another, may set in. If we are inclined toward melancholia, we might give ourselves over to long, brooding thoughts about how sad it is that things never seem to turn out just as we thought they would, meaning, they turn out *less* than we thought they would. These experiences lead us to wonder: Can any of our desires ever be completely and permanently satisfied?

Desire can be frustrated, whenever a loved object, despite our best efforts, eludes us. We can devote much time and energy to pursuing goods that we never come to possess. Things could have gone differently for Wally regarding one of the objects of his desire. The gal who, he was convinced, was just like the gal that married dear old dad, could have given him the cold shoulder and turned a deaf ear to his matrimonial entreaties. All his most earnest efforts along those lines could have gone for nought.

When a desire is fulfilled and a loved object obtained, we experience, as noted, a period of quiet contentment, and that particular desire is gone. But no sooner does it take its leave than another desire promptly moves in to take its place. Even when we come into the possession of objects with which we remain generally pleased and satisfied, desire, fixing itself on entirely new objects now, continues to assert itself. Its fires will never be extinguished. The gal Wally was pursuing, just like the one that married dear old dad—her name was Gloria, by the way—batted her beautiful brown eyes, lowered her perfectly coiffured head, and breathed a definitive "Yes." They were married and lived happily ever after. Does that mean that Wally and Gloria henceforth experience no desire? The question should answer itself.

Perhaps the most arresting form human desire can take is when we cannot give any precise identity to its object. Lallita is a lady who can say, "I have everything that I have ever wanted," and honestly mean it. Yet, for all that, there remains a desire for something she cannot quite put her finger on, for which she doesn't have a name. It is unusual, as a desire, because there is nothing clamorous about it. It is persistent, yet quietly so, not pushily intrusive. It rests in her as a vague, low-toned yearning for she knows-not-what. Strangely, she feels that her inability to give it an exact name has, somehow, something to do with its identity. Lallita often thinks about all the goods she has pursued, and has come to possess. "What was it in them," she muses, "what shared character did they have, that drew me to them? What made all these many and various goods seem good to me?"

Eight

Is There an Overall End?

All of our lives are packed solid with a multitude of ends, which tells us why we are the nonstop activists that we are. We're always on the go, in the pursuit of goods. Now is the time to pose a pointed question: Might there be something that could qualify as an overall end, an end to end all ends, as it were? If an end is the ultimate explanation for all the particular ends toward which action is directed, we call that the overall end. It is what accounts for all of our actions taken together, the governing reason for our doing whatever it is we do.

What would such an end look like? It would be an "all stops here" end, which is to say, self-sufficient. It would not point to anything beyond itself. It would not be the kind of end which, once achieved, is then transmogrified into a means for attaining something yet further down the road. And, since it is self-sufficient, its possession would bring with it, at least, an adequate degree of satisfaction.

By way of addressing the question whether or not there is such an overall end, I propose the following imagined scenario. I take a poll of all adults now living on the face of the earth. My poll is very simple, for it contains what is essentially a single question. However, in order to make sure the people polled understood what I am trying to get at, I decided to frame the question in three different ways, as follows: (1) "What one thing in life do you want more than anything else?" (2) "What above all else are you looking for in life?" (3) "Why do you do whatever you do?" Of the responses I received, almost all of them were expressed in either one word or in three: "Happiness"; "To be happy." I therefore concluded that it is happiness which people want more than anything else; it is what they are most looking for in life; it is the ultimate explanation for why they do whatever they do. It is the overall end.

A fictional poll does not provide us with conclusive scientific proof that the overall end of human action, that which is the ultimate explanation for whatever we do, is happiness. Even so, were such a poll actually taken, it would not be preposterous to suggest that most people would likely cite happiness as what they most desire. But now, putting fictional polls aside, let us reflect on the matter in specific, experiential terms, in *personal* terms. Is not happiness *the* end which all of us are seeking? Is not happiness the overriding explanation for everything we do? Think about your own life, your own actions, *all* of them, everything you do or ever have done, consciously and deliberately. Every act you perform is calculated to gain something which you desire, and you desire it because you perceive it as good, and you perceive it as good because you have persuaded yourself that the desired good, once gained, is going to make your condition better off than it was before the good was in your possession; its possession, in other words, is going to contribute, in greater or lesser degree, to your happiness.

Each and every act, in the final analysis, is performed for the sake of happiness. Happiness is what human behavior is ultimately all about, for it is precisely for the sake of happiness that all particular ends are pursued; it is the governing purpose which bestows value upon all of them. Given its commanding importance, it is incumbent upon us to consider this idea of happiness more closely.

Nine
The Idea of Happiness

Happiness qualifies as the overall end, the final end, because it is self-suffi-cient. There is nothing above it or beyond it that could be the proper object of our desire. It is the *final* end because it does not serve as a means whose purpose is to achieve any further end. Happiness is that toward which all human action is directed, at which all human aspiration stops. "Why do you want to be happy?" That would count as a very silly question. It seeks for reasons where no reasons need be sought. To ask why we want to be happy implies that happiness is for something beyond happiness. But it isn't. Happiness is for itself. We want to be happy simply because we want to be happy, for happiness's own sweet, completely satisfying sake.

Happiness is the *ne plus ultra*, the tops, the very pinnacle, the definitive desideratum. The idea of happiness brings with it the sense of completion. While perhaps being prepared to grant all that, still, on the basis of our own real life experiences with happiness, we would want to make some qualifications, saying things like, "Completion? Yes, of sorts, up to a point." The much-used term "complete happiness" indicates that there is a less-than-complete kind. This phenomenon we call happiness admits of degrees. Happiness might be what we are all seeking in whatever we do, but do we ever find it in a pure, unadulterated form? Are we ever perfectly content with the ends we have achieved? It would seem not. This recalls what we were saying earlier about the nature of desire. Is not the fact that we are never free of desire a pretty sure sign that whatever happiness we manage to achieve is never perfect happiness? Would not a person who had attained a state of perfect happiness be a person without desire? If one were in such a state, what more could one desire? It would seem then that the best we can hope for, as was suggested earlier, is the highest degree of happiness possible, a state in which we experience the greatest amount of content-ment, and the least amount of nagging desire. Let us say that we are reasonably content with the situation in which we now find ourselves, but we would be hesitant to claim that we are completely satisfied, meaning that there is nothing more to be desired, to aspire after.

The gaining of a specific good can contribute to one's happiness, but it does not take much experience in living to realize the fallaciousness of the reasoning which would have it that, the more goods gained, the deeper, the more complete the happiness for the gainer of those goods. Happiness, at bottom, does not consist so much in *having* in a certain way as in *being* in a certain way. Freighted phrases like "the pursuit of happiness" can lure us into thinking about happiness too much in terms of its being something "out there," an objective "something" of sorts, a definable state, that we have to be constantly chasing after. Now, though happiness is not something "out there," it has very much to do with what is out there, in the sense that it is directly dependent upon the actions in which we engage in the real world.

Ten

Is Happiness One Thing?

Yet more must be said on the subject of happiness. I remind you of my imaginary world-wide poll, the results of which justified the conclusion that the preponderance of people take happiness to be the overall end of human action, the basic explanation for everything we do. Bear with me now as I continue my imaginative musings. After collecting and registering the results of that first poll, I then took a second. This poll too had but one question, and in this case I managed to give it single, short expression: "What do you mean by 'happiness'?" If the responses to the first poll showed a remarkable consensus of opinion, those of the second were a confusing babble of wildly conflicting views. The general conclusion I drew from the polls was this: while everyone wants to be happy, there seems to be no common agreement as to what being happy means. People define happiness in a variety of ways.

We have a problem on our hands. It appeared for a moment there, by identifying happiness as the overall end, that we had found a promising unifying idea, offering something like a blanket explanation for all human behavior. If happiness is indeed what everyone seeks, if it is the root reason behind everything we do, then we have an idea around which we can feasibly build a coherent ethical theory. But it is hard to build a coherent theory around an idea which is itself not coherent, and if there are multiple meanings attached to happiness, that idea would seem to lack coherence.

The conclusion to that line of reasoning is not justified. There is no reason to scuttle happiness as a pivotal idea for ethics. An idea cannot be said to lack coherence because people have disparate opinions regarding it. It might very well be just those disparate opinions which are, if not exactly incoherent, at least confused. That, in fact, is the case. Two things are to be observed regarding what I will call the principal misapprehensions about the nature of happiness. (1) There really are not that many misapprehensions, only a handful in fact, and they are as old, it would appear, as the race itself. Their longevity and their endurance suggests that we human beings do not have much originality when it comes to figuring out the nature of happiness. We unimaginatively fall into the same well-worn stock of fallacies down through the ages. (2) Here we are confronted with misapprehensions, and serious ones, concerning the nature of happiness, but what is proposed in each case is not altogether irrational; far from it. One of the classic misapprehensions, which we will be examining along with others in the next chapter, has it that happiness consists in riches, in having an abundance of material goods. This is not wrong-headed because there is something inherently bad about material goods; in fact, they constitute a real good. The mistake here is one of radical misplacement, of giving primacy of place to what is of secondary importance.

But now let us consider some of the principal misapprehensions about the nature of happiness.

Eleven

Various Misapprehensions
Regarding the Nature of Happiness

"If only I were rich, then I would be happy. Not filthy rich, mind you. I don't want to be vulgar about it, nor ostentatious. No conspicuous consumption, understand, or anything like that. I just want to be, let us say, adequately rich, comfortably rich, to have enough money to allow me to carry on through life contentedly, completely free of any financial worries, snug and secure in my own domain, tending my lush little garden, until death do we part. Let me put it this way: I'd like to have enough money so that I won't ever have to think about money."

"You want to know what I think it would take to make me happy, really happy, as in perfectly content and satisfied? It's power. Power! I want power. I want it first of all for myself, to ensure my complete and unfettered independence, so that I will no longer have to put up with people who are constantly telling me how to lead my life, so I can prevent people from constantly encroaching on my territory. Don't get me wrong, this isn't just a reckless ego trip for me, but I have to put the main emphasis where it belongs. First, I've got to take care of myself, get power for myself. If that doesn't happen, then I'll be in no position to empower other people, do you see? I'm a man of ideas, big ideas, and once I get power I can put those ideas to work, straighten out other people's lives, straighten out the whole system. Give me power and I'd be happy, and I'd make other people happy too. Believe me."

"What do I most want out of life? What do I think I would need in order to be happy? Not much, really. All I'm looking for is a little recognition and appreciation of myself in terms of who I really am, an honest acknowledgment of what I've succeeded in accomplishing. Respect? Well, all right, I'll admit it. That's what I want. What's wrong with wanting a little respect, some sensitive awareness, on the part of others, of me as a person, an appreciative recognition of my talents and what I've done with them? I'm not asking for the world with a fence around it. My needs are modest. I would be happy, quite happy, with a decent amount of respect."

"How do I spell happiness? H-e-a-l-t-h. Let me have my health, let this body of mine be kept free of anything that would debilitate it, which would prevent it from not working in the wonderfully well way it is working for me now, and you can have all the rest—money, clout, sex, fame, whatever. After all, what good would all that stuff do me if I didn't have my health? Money? All the money in the world is not going to buy me health. It's a cliché, I know, but who's going to argue with it? To me, my health is the most precious thing in the world. With it, I'm happy. Without it, I'd be miserable."

"Let the good times roll, twenty-four-seven—that's my idea of happiness. So long as I'm having fun, the skies are nothing but blue, the sun's always shining. It's a mental thing, really, a frame of mind, an attitude. Let's be realistic. Life is short, as the sage says. Truisms tend to be true. And as far as I'm concerned we're here to enjoy ourselves, have a good time, wring the most pleasure we can out of this otherwise lousy life. That's Rule Number One. Rule Number Two is: avoid pain, all pain. We can't afford to be morbid, and it's morbid to get mixed up with pain. It's no good for the attitude. Hey, there's no mystery here, no secret formula. You want to be happy? Have fun!"

Consider the above statements to be culled from the responses I got from my second imaginary poll. Let them serve as a representative sample. Each of those responses should sound familiar, even hackneyed, and that is instructive. Summing up the above responses in a word or two, happiness is said to be chiefly founded in: (1) riches, or material goods; (2) power; (3) reputation; (4) health; (5) pleasure. A more detailed analysis of our poll would no doubt permit me to lengthen the list somewhat, but, as already noted, those five categories reflect what a great many people reckon happiness to be essentially all about, not just today, but, so the evidence from history shows, perennially. If we were to consult a work Aristotle wrote some two and a half millennia ago, his *Ethics*, we would come across a list pretty close to the one spelled out above. As the French say, the more things change, the more they stay the same.

The purpose of Aristotle's list was to show how we typically get it wrong when it comes to figuring out what happiness is all about. Riches, power, honor, health, pleasure—these all count as inadequate notions of happiness. To hitch your wagon to any one of them, power, say, dedicating yourself exclusively to it, making it the number one aim behind all you do, that for which essentially you live, is to have seriously misapprehended the nature of happiness.

But what, one might legitimately ask, is the problem? Is there anything essentially wrong with any one of these things? No, there isn't. In fact, there's something essentially right about all of them. Consider each in turn. Riches, or let us say, material goods, are not only important for a happy life, in a way they are necessary to it. Thinking in minimalist terms, happiness would not be possible without adequate food, clothing, and shelter. But how about riches? There is no intrinsic incompatibility between being rich and being truly happy, which is to say, living an ethical life. It is not simply being rich that tells the tale, but how one is rich, i.e., how one uses one's riches.

Because we are all painfully aware of the ways in which power can be abused, sometimes flagrantly, even brutally, we might tend to leap to the conclusion that there is something inherently evil in power. Therefore, actively to seek power would be unethical. This is poor thinking. Power, in the most elementary sense, is simply the capacity to act efficiently, and if we did not have that capacity, that is, if we were bereft of power, it would be impossible for us to be ethical. As with riches, the problem is not with power as such, but with how it is employed, the direction we give to our capacities.

Should we be beating our breasts over the fact that we have the desire to be respected, to be the recipients on occasion of some recognition and appreciation on the part of others? No. But like every other legitimate desire, it can be given exaggerated importance. It is tedious to have to listen to those who bemoan what they consider to be the unforgivable fact that they "don't get no respect," as if the universe owed them a special debt. But we should not condemn a legitimate concern because of the ways it can be twisted out of shape. Ideally, every single human being, simply on the basis of being such, is deserving of respect. It's not wrong to want respect. On the other hand, however, there is no irreparable damage done to our genuine happiness if we don't get it.

And who is going to contest the importance of health, and the part it can play in our happiness? It is not only commendable for us to tend conscientiously to our health, we have an obligation to do so. But though health plays a part in happiness, it is not equivalent to happiness, and therefore it is a false equation to say that loss of health = loss of happiness.

Pleasure? It is good. Pain is evil. No argument there. Pleasure has a critically important role to play in ethics, and we will have more to say about it later. For now I will simply make the obvious observation that pleasure can sometimes be problematic. That happens when we allow it to become the central factor of our lives. Pleasure, the proverb has it, makes a heavenly servant, but a hellish master.

Given the fact that happiness deserves to be considered the final end, the definitive explanation for everything we do, when we get confused about its true nature it is because we get confused about ends and means. Wealth, power, honor, health, pleasure: what role, exactly, should these be playing in our lives? They should all function as means, not ends. We must not permit any one of them to represent what our life is centrally all about. No one of them is worthy of being the governing factor in our lives.

This is clear enough with regard to wealth and power. The world's literature is replete with tragic tales about people who made riches or power the end-all and be-all of their lives. The obsessive concern for riches turns into a greed that eats away at the soul; the disordered desire for power ends up as an all-consuming lust. The Midas touch becomes the touch of death. The lust for power can lead to rapaciousness of monstrous proportions, a fact which the history of the human race gives us a surfeit of sad examples.

But how can we go wrong by being concerned about our health? By fostering an unhealthy concern for our health, and we do that by making it an end in itself. Health, like power, is a means to happiness, not the very stuff of happiness. We should want to be healthy not simply to be healthy, but so that, as healthy, we can do our jobs, efficiently meet the obligations our state in life places upon us. To make a fetish of health is a form of self-indulgence. *Mens sana in corpore sano*, the ancient Romans used to say, "A healthy mind in a healthy body." An unhealthy mind in a healthy body is a combination that serves neither mind nor body. Like pleasure, health is a good and a necessary thing, but not the only thing.

We are now ready to close in on a definition of happiness that will serve as our pivotal idea for a sound ethical theory. But first we have to deal with an argument that threatens to undermine everything that I have said so far.

Twelve

Objections!

The approach to ethics I have been taking up to this point displays, rather prominently, what is known as a eudemonic, or eudemonistic, emphasis. Those two fifty-dollar terms trace their origins back to a Greek word, *eudaimonia*, which means "happiness." By putting the kind of stress I have on the idea of happiness, I have been obliquely recognizing it as a pivotal idea for ethics.

But there are some philosophers who would take vigorous exception to this whole approach, contending that happiness should not, in fact, play the role that I have assigned to it. The opposition party we have to contend with here is not, as it happens, unified, and there are two distinct positions we need to consider.

The basic thrust of the first position is as follows. To give primacy of place to the idea of happiness in ethics denigrates this noble science of morals, and turns it into a tawdry program for the advancement of a narrow-minded egotism. Happiness cannot be held up as the goal of all human endeavor, the explanatory purpose behind all of our actions. To see why this is so, we need only remind ourselves of the essential nature of happiness: it is a pleasurable state of mind. Such being the case, the much publicized "pursuit of happiness" is tantamount to the pursuit of pleasure, and the so-called ethical person thus becomes someone whose principal concern is ensuring his own self-centered gratification. But self-centered gratification is not the purpose of human action. An authentic ethics is altruistic; it looks outward, not inward. Genuine ethical behavior is not selfish behavior.

The cogency of this argument turns on the soundness of the idea of happiness by which it is informed. If happiness is in essence, as claimed, one and the same with pleasure, then the argument would have real teeth to it, and the position we are taking here would be deservedly chewed to pieces by it. However, happiness is not what the argument claims it to be.

Though happiness may, at times, be associated with a state of mind marked by placid contentment—certainly a pleasant enough state to be in—it is not to be equated with such a state. Happiness can involve pleasure, and often does, but it is not the same thing as pleasure.

The second position is considerably more sophisticated. It does not reduce happiness to pleasure, and freely acknowledges that it plays an important role in ethics, but, like the first position, it is unwilling to allow that happiness should be the principal impetus for human action. The advocates of this position put great stress on the importance of the unconditional nature of ethical behavior. I can be said to perform any act unconditionally when I perform it simply because it is a good act. It is the sheer goodness of the act that makes it imperative that I perform it. I do not set any conditions for the performance of the act, do not look for anything outside of the act itself in order to justify my performing it. I do not reason hypothetically or conditionally regarding it, that is, I do not say: "If I can be confident that Act X will yield positive effects, such as happiness, then I will perform Act X, but only under that condition." So, happiness becomes a condition to be met for acting ethically, but again, there should be no conditions set for acting ethically, not even the possibility that by so acting we will be made happy.

If I were to reason and act in the way this position opposes, I would be tentative whereas I should be determined, vacillating whereas I should be resolute and decisive, and that would not be the mark of a genuinely ethical person. I am thinking soundly, when it comes to ethics, only when I give myself clear, unambiguous, *unconditional* imperatives. If Act X is a good act, the right kind of thing to do, then that's all I need to know, and I must tell myself, "Do it! with no ifs, ands, or buts." While this position, as noted, recognizes the importance of happiness for ethics, it is reluctant to grant it the place we want for it. One reason for this is that it regards the very idea of happiness as problematic on account of the fact that it is so difficult to define, thus engendering all sorts of disagreement over its essential nature.

How should we respond to this second position? We do not want to contest the notion that if a particular act can be determined to be the right thing to do, then it should be done, period. No conditions should be attached to its performance. But the advocates of this position are mistaken in thinking that in a eudemonic ethics happiness is being set up as the condition for doing a good act. This is not the case. We do not establish happiness as something outside and apart from the act itself. As we shall see, there is no separation between good action and happiness. We do not act well in order to be happy; acting well and happiness are one and the same thing.

We must now take a closer look at the relation between acting well, being ethical in the most general sense, and happiness.

Thirteen
What Is Happiness?

A review. We have already made a number of important points concerning the nature of happiness. First and foremost, we assert that happiness is a final end, the motivating purpose which calls every human act into existence. An end, we know, is the explanation for any particular action. Hitting the bull's-eye is the end, the purpose, behind shooting an arrow at a target. An unqualifiedly final end is, as it were, the end of all particular ends, the ultimate explanation for all our actions, the "last word" reason for everything we do, including something as prosaic as shooting arrows at targets. We have also called this the overall end.

We can easily see how happiness meets the requirements for a final end. "Because I want to be happy," or words to that effect, is the response which we would be most likely to give if we were pressed to name the *one* reason that best accounts for the sum total of our behavior. If we reflect on even the most trivial things which we do with conscious intent, digging deeply into our memory to find their primal motivating principle, their root cause, we would unearth a desire for happiness.

Very closely bound up with the idea of happiness as a final end is the idea that it is something that is sought for its own sake, and so we call it self-sufficient. We do not prize happiness as if it were some kind of way station which, once arrived at, then becomes the point of departure for something more desirable that lies somewhere ahead. Happiness is the terminus. It is just where we want to be. As *final* end, it does not transmute into a means to yet another end. Given this particular feature of happiness, the fitting response to its possession would be a deep-seated sense of satisfaction. If we are happy we are content, at peace with ourselves and our general situation.

Though I have not given the point much emphasis thus far, another key feature of happiness as we are defining it is the fact that it must be permanent. But is anything permanent in this life? If we are speaking of absolute permanence, that is something which, it must be conceded, is not within our capacities to secure. What I have in mind here is relative permanence. A house is a permanent dwelling in comparison to a tent, and one thinks of well-constructed houses that have been in the same family for generations. Happiness must be stable and enduring. Like a tent, it should not be able to be struck in a matter of a few minutes. True, even a well-constructed house can burn down, or be demolished by a tornado, but barring catastrophic events of that order, it is going to be there waiting for us when we come home at the end of the day, day after day. It is that kind of abiding stability we look for in happiness. Happiness is permanent in the sense that it should last as long as the person who possesses it.

Besides those already discussed, we need to call attention to another common way of regarding happiness which is not all that helpful in conveying its true nature. We often talk about happiness in quantitative terms, treating it as some kind of commodity that could be increased or diminished in a precisely calculable way, as if adding to our happiness would be like adding to our bank account. A likely explanation for our thinking along those lines may lie in the tendency to link happiness with material possessions. It is more appropriate to think of the kind of augmentation that pertains to happiness in terms of intensification or perfection, as takes place when the playing of a musical instrument is perfected by continuous and conscientious practice. So, then, what is happiness? First, to repeat a point made earlier, happiness is not something external to ourselves; it is not separate from the actions that achieve it. I now propose an idea of happiness which will very likely be quite foreign to you, and therefore you will have to give it some careful thought to appreciate its poignancy. Happiness is action, the action of being ethical. I have given much stress to the fact that happiness is the end of action; but for all that it is not separate from action. Happiness is one and the same as the action. A person has happiness, *is* happy, because of the way the person acts, by pursuing the good, acting ethically. The person's happiness and ethical actions are identical.

Our lives might be thought of as elaborate edifices, and our accumulated actions as the material by which they are constructed. What we are, as persons, is revealed by how we act. Happiness is *a special state of being,* a particular way of living. To grasp the essence of happiness, to grasp its existential reality, we need to focus all our attention on the individual, the acting human person whom we identify as *being* happy.

What principally founds our identification of a particular person as happy? Who is the truly happy human being? It is the person who acts consistently and reliably in a way which is in accord with and reflects what is truly good, meaning that which is in accord with and reflects man's rational nature. The consistency of behavior here underscores the element of permanence. Aristotle, who is the originator of the idea of happiness I have been developing, defined happiness very simply and poignantly as a life lived according to virtue.

Consider a specific virtue, justice. A happy person is one who habitually, as a matter of course, acts justly, *and his happiness consists in* acting in precisely that way. There is a merger between being just and being happy. Because the virtues are all consistent with one another, the person whose actions habitually reflect justice would habitually reflect all the other virtues as well, albeit in varying degrees. There is therefore a qualitative similarity among all the actions of the person, and because all the actions of any one of us can be said to constitute a summary statement of what we essentially are, we repeat the point made above, that happiness is, at bottom, a way of being, a way of living one's human life. Happiness cannot be divorced from the person who is happy, hence the permanency of happiness earlier alluded to.

Happiness consists in living our lives in a certain way—ethically, i.e., in accordance with virtue—and therefore we are happy precisely because of that way of living. Happiness is not something that falls out of the sky on us. It is something we ourselves bring about by the way we freely choose to behave. We do not live according to virtue in order to gain happiness; living according to virtue *is* happiness. It is futile to regard happiness as "out there." If we succeed in achieving happiness, we will find it in only one place, in ourselves—more exactly, in what we do, in how we consistently behave over the course of our lives.

A common misconception about happiness is to suppose that it is necessarily associated with positive emotions. A happy person may or may or not at any one time experience positive emotions, but that is incidental. Happiness does not of course preclude positive emotions, but they do not necessarily accompany it. There are certain people who are cheerful and upbeat by temperament, but who may not be happy in the way we have defined it. Happiness is not decided by temperament; if it were, it would be something genetically determined, and therefore beyond our control. A very important aspect of happiness is the fact that it is under our control, precisely in the way, and to the extent, that our actions are under our control.

It would be to trivialize happiness to reduce it to a matter of our "feeling good about oneself," given the connotations usually attached to that phrase. The accent, for a happy person, is not upon feeling positively but upon acting positively. If good feelings happen to accompany good action, that is always a welcome additive, and one would be churlish not to accept such feelings with gratitude. But in the final analysis the good feelings are of secondary importance, and in some instances simply irrelevant. The attitude espoused by the ethical position we described previously, holding that we must do the right thing, however we might feel about it, is an altogether commendable attitude.

But have I not, in stressing the intimate bond that exists between happiness and action, given insufficient attention to the idea of happiness as a state of mind? Happiness may be considered a state of mind, but we should draw out the implications of doing so. States of mind are brought about and defined by our actions. Happiness, then, as a state of mind, is established by, and inseparable from, the kind of action which is identical with happiness. When we are happy we are thoroughly at peace with ourselves by reason of our being true to our proper nature, that is, for living up to what we are as rational beings.

Fourteen

Action and Happiness Are One

How is it that happiness is one and the same with action? It would be worth our while to press that question, for, given the way we generally tend to think about happiness, the idea that it is to be identified with a certain kind of action is not one that immediately leaps into the mind. The road to greater clarity on this important point is a short one, and can be traversed in three simple steps. Let us proceed.

The first step is an exercise in memory, regarding the nature of an individual act. I hope that by this time it is one of our more firmly established convictions that every act is for the sake of an end. It is of the very nature of an act to be purposeful; if it were not so, it simply would not qualify as an act. Granting that much, we see that it is the end which defines the act, drawing it out of what would otherwise be a vague, indeterminate state—motion without meaning—and conferring upon it a clearly recognizable, hence nameable, identity. The end "locates" the act, invests it with the kind of specificity which allows it to be distinguished from other acts. It is a loaf of bread, on the one hand, and Yvonne's saying "Yes" to Damian, on the other, that distinguish the act of baking bread from the act of making a marriage proposal.

Step two. Just as the end defines the act, the act, in turn, defines the agent or actor, the originating source of the act. How so? Well, actually, in all sorts of possible ways, depending on the nature of the act and the role it plays in the overall behavior of the agent. If baking bread is more than a sometime diversion for Ruth, is an activity she regularly engages in, is, moreover, the means by which she makes a living, we would then identify Ruth with the activity of baking, and call her a baker. The general condition or status of a person is established, then subsequently altered in one way or another, by the actions performed by the person. Sometimes just a single act, if weighty enough, can dramatically alter someone's status. The proximate result of an accepted marriage proposal is a change in status of the parties concerned, from "single" to "engaged," which latter status will eventually be replaced by "married."

Step three. What we call happiness, I think we would all agree, is a certain condition or state in which people find themselves. I referred to it earlier as a state of mind. Because conditions or states of mind are created and preserved by the actions we perform, we should be able to see the very close connection between happiness and action. We might want to look upon the relation between the two in terms of cause and effect, where the action brings about the condition. If so, we need to be aware that the cause/effect relation at work here is of a peculiarly close kind.

There are certain causes which, once they have completed their causative chore, can retire from active duty so to speak, while the effect they have instigated continues. A golfer can drive a golf ball off the tee and then, his swing complete, stand there motionless and watch the ball, a contented smile playing upon his lips, as it soars into the fresh morning air right down the middle of the fairway. The golf ball's continuing motion does not depend on the golfer's continuing motion.

Not far from the tee, a groundskeeper pushes a wheelbarrow down a sinuous pathway. The wheelbarrow moves and the groundskeeper moves, but the wheelbarrow moves only so long as the groundskeeper does the moving. Should the motion of the groundskeeper stop, so too would the motion of the wheelbarrow. The wheelbarrow's condition, being in a state of motion, depends directly upon the continuing action of the groundskeeper.

The kind of cause/effect relation described in the second example, involving the wheelbarrow and the groundskeeper, is the kind that applies to the relation that exists between happiness and the action that causes it. The continuation of the condition depends on the continuation of the action. But the example is imperfect in two respects. The distinction between wheelbarrow and groundskeeper is more marked than that between happiness and the action that causes it; indeed, it is a separation. There is no separation between the acting person and the condition brought about by his action. Moreover, the action necessary to ensure the continuity of a state of happiness is not continuous in the same way as is that of the groundskeeper as he keeps the wheelbarrow moving along the pathway. When we say, regarding happiness, that its maintenance requires continuous action, all we mean is that there must be a consistent pattern of a certain type of activity sustained over time, not that the happy person is involved in nonstop activity. Even happy people have to get some sleep.

In sum, to be happy is to be in a condition that is brought about and preserved on a continuing basis by a certain kind of behavior habitually engaged in by a person who is in that condition. The behavior is identical with the condition in the sense that, no behavior, no condition. And what kind of behavior is that? It is virtuous behavior. To act consistently in accordance with virtue means, understood in the most fundamental sense, to act in a fully human fashion, to fulfill oneself as a person, as a rational animal. That is what it means to be happy. At the risk of being tediously repetitive, I must articulate yet once again a key point. Happiness does not so much follow from acting in a certain way as it *consists* in acting in a certain way. Put more pointedly, virtuous acts are done for their own sake. The value of doing them is found in the very doing of them.

Fifteen
The Human Act

Happiness consists in a certain type of action, which we have generically described as virtuous action, but all human action, whatever its particular kind, is reducible to the individual act. If we want to get an accurate reading of a particular kind of action, then we have to focus on the individual act that contributes to the composition of that kind of action, and try to determine what it is about. Knowledge of the constituent parts (individual acts) will provide us with critical information about the nature of the whole (kind of action) which is constituted by the parts.

Earlier, in an attempt to pin down a precise understanding of human behavior, we described it as purposeful behavior, behavior that is conscious and deliberate in its end-pursuing efforts. When we act humanly, in the most basic sense of the term, we act intentionally, pursuing particular ends while in the process being fully aware of the ends precisely as ends, i.e., as what we are aiming to achieve. Our end-oriented activity, as human, does not find its root explanation in raw, instinctual urges. We do have, to be sure, raw, instinctual urges, but when they are the driving impetus behind our actions we are not acting humanly. If primal instincts were what principally and regularly drove human behavior, it would indeed be a jungle out there, and most of us would opt to stay indoors, perhaps peeking through the blinds occasionally to register the latest outrage taking place.

As human agents, we are conscious of ends precisely as ends because of the fusion that takes place in our minds between the end and the good. We pursue any given end because we *conceptualize* it as something which, if attained, will accrue to our benefit; in other words, we regard it as a good. Furthermore, we can imagine the possible success of our pursuit, sometimes in a very detailed way, even though the pursuit may in fact turn out to be a failure.

The individual human act is obviously going to be found nowhere else but in the larger context of human behavior considered as a whole, of which it is a constituent part, and that allows us immediately to identify it as an act that is conscious and deliberate. Please note the specialized way in which we are employing the phrase "human act." A *human* act is, by definition, a conscious and deliberate act. An alternate name for "human act," which makes explicit what is at issue here, is "voluntary act." The two terms, "human act" and "voluntary act," are synonymous. The voluntary act is the only act which is of interest to us in ethics, for unless an act is voluntary— i.e., conscious and deliberate, done intentionally to achieve a specific end— it is not open to the peculiar kind of assessment with which ethics occupies itself.

And the peculiar kind of assessment with which ethics occupies itself? In a word, *moral* assessment. We judge any particular act to be either morally good or bad, and thus attach to it either praise or blame, not on the basis of its being a good or bad athletic act, or musical act, or legal act, or bridge-playing act, but only on the basis of its being a good or bad human act. We ask of the act: Does it or does it not measure up to the standards according to which we can with confidence call it simply "human," that is, the type of act one should expect from a rational agent? But we have no warrant for asking such a question unless we have first satisfactorily answered a question that must necessarily precede it: Was the act voluntary? If the answer to that question is negative, everything stops right there as far as the moral assessment of the act is concerned. No ethical issue is obviously at stake.

Given the importance of the voluntary act, it is well that we familiarize ourselves with its essential features. There are two conditions that have to be met before an act can qualify as a voluntary act: (1) the agent must know what he is doing; (2) the agent must will what he is doing.

To say that an agent must know what he is doing is not simply to assert that he must be conscious—that goes without saying—but that he must be conscious of the exact nature of the act he is performing, and of its consequences. An example to illustrate this important point would be helpful. Manfred, a college professor, was leaving the Science Building at 2:00 a.m. one morning after spending many laborious hours in the lab. As he made his way sleepily down the hallway he noticed that all the lights in the botany lab were ablaze. He stopped at the door and looked through the glass, but could see no one. He opened the door and called out, "Anyone here?" No answer. "Thoughtless," he thought to himself, "wasting electricity like that." After flicking off all the lights, he continued on his way, feeling mildly virtuous for performing a good conservationist deed.

It was only the following day that Manfred learned that his apparent good deed had brought about disastrous results. The special type of lights that had been installed in the botany lab had been left on for a purpose, and were intended to be kept burning twenty-four hours a day for a period of fourteen days, as part of a delicate, heavily funded experiment having to do with a rare species of Ecuadorian flora, which was being conducted by Dr. Francisco Flores, Associate Professor of Botany. As a result of the blackout imposed by Manfred, the experiment was ruined. Thousands of dollars in grant money went down the drain, along with a possible promotion for Dr. Flores had the experiment turned out successfully.

Manfred was devastated by what he had done, and not without reason. It was his action, after all, that had ruined the experiment. But was he intending to ruin a costly experiment by turning off the lights? Not at all. More pointedly, did he *know* he was doing that by turning off the lights? He did not. If Manfred had been aware of the consequences of his turning off the lights, and if, with those consequences in mind, he had turned off the lights deliberately, then we would have quite a different situation on our hands. As it was, because Manfred was unaware of the exact nature of his action, he cannot be said to be morally responsible for it. He was conscious of the fact that he was turning off the lights, but he was not conscious of the fact that, by doing so, he was ruining an experiment, and in that respect it would be accurate to say that he did not know what he was doing. His act was involuntary. He is not guilty of unethical behavior.

A couple of incidental observations on the type of situation just described would be in order. The fact that someone is not morally culpable for an act which has negative consequences does not of course mean that the person may not feel badly about his performing the act. Manfred, as noted, was a very sad scientist when he realized what he had done. But feeling bad about a deed one has done does not mean that the deed itself, viewed from an ethical point of view, was bad. That is a rather obvious point, but worth mentioning nonetheless, for sometimes we mistake feeling guilty for being guilty. Second observation: the fact that a person is not morally culpable for a deed does not mean that he cannot be found legally culpable for it, especially in a lasciviously litigious society such as our own.

We will consider another example, bearing upon the critically important factor of voluntariness. It was mid-afternoon when Loreen received the phone call at the real estate agency where she worked. It was a male voice, but it was muffled, and at first she could not make out the words. But the message was repeated three times, and eventually she got it. When she set down the phone she was visibly trembling. The voice had told her that if she wanted to see her daughter alive again she was to put twenty-five thousand dollars, in cash, in a paper bag and then deposit the bag in a designated locker at the Greyhound bus depot. This was to be done no later than 7:00 p.m. If she were to contact the police, or anyone else, about this matter, she could be assured that she had already seen her daughter for the last time. She had listened spellbound. As soon as she found her voice she began to ask rapid-fire questions, but by way of reply all she heard was the dial tone buzzing monotonously in her ear.

Was this some kind of cruel hoax? A bit panicky now, she called the day-care center where she had left her daughter that morning. Mrs. Hawkins, who ran the center, explained, noticeably surprised by the inquiry, that no, Janice was not there. She had been picked up about a half-hour ago by Natalie, who identified herself as Loreen's best friend. Loreen's blood went cold. She had no friend, best or otherwise, by the name of Natalie. She asked Mrs. Hawkins to describe the woman. She described a stranger. Loreen's voice was cracking when she put down the receiver.

It was no hoax. Loreen told her boss that something had suddenly come up and she had to leave work early. She would explain later. She drove directly to her bank, where she had in her savings account the amount of $26,331.75—all the money she had to her name. She withdrew $25,000 in cash, put it in a large manila envelope, drove to the bus depot, and deposited it in locker 4610, and, as she had been instructed, put the key to the locker in the water closet of the toilet in the stall farthest from the door in the women's washroom. She then went home and waited. Fifty-five minutes later the phone rang. It was the same muffled male voice she had heard on her office phone. The voice told her that they got the money. She should now go to the intersection of 46th Street and Snelling Avenue. There was a bus stop shelter on the northwest corner. Her daughter would be in the shelter. Loreen drove to the specified intersection, her heart thudding against her ribs. She found her daughter sitting on the bench of the shelter, swinging her legs back and forth, chewing away on a large stick of red licorice. When she saw her mother she broke into a big, toothy grin. She was unharmed, and apparently quite unfazed by her kidnaping. Loreen was hugely relieved, but it was with not a little bitterness that she recalled the last words spoken by the muffled voice on the phone: "Have a nice day."

How are we to assess Loreen's actions from a moral point of view? I think that we would all agree that she did the right thing, perhaps the only thing she could have done under the circumstances. But the reason I recount this tawdry episode is to raise a question concerning the precise nature of Loreen's actions. Were they voluntary? Did she act freely when she withdrew twenty-five thousand dollars from the bank and turn it over to some thoroughly despicable people? We will answer the question with both Yes and No. In one sense, what she did, she did knowingly and willingly. But her actions could not be said to have been free without qualification. We ask ourselves: If the circumstances had been different from what they actually were, would Loreen have acted in the way she did? The answer is clearly No. It was the circumstances that forced her hand, and she acted in a way in which she otherwise very definitely would not have acted. She was coerced to do what she did, and that coercion qualified the freedom with which she acted. Her actions, therefore, could not be said to have been voluntary in the fullest sense.

How would we analyze a situation in which a person is coerced, either physically or psychologically, to commit a crime? What if Loreen's caller had instructed her to *rob* a bank? And what if Loreen, desperate for her child's safety, carried out the caller's instructions and delivered the stolen cash to the kidnappers? Would she be morally culpable for her actions? Settling that question correctly turns on the critical factor of coercion. We will leave it to the courts to sort out the legal niceties of the situation, but looking at it from a moral point of view, because Loreen acted under coercion we can assume that she did not act voluntarily. If that assumption is justified (something that can only be determined by examining all the particulars of the case), then she is morally innocent.

To sum up. No act is subject to moral assessment unless it is a voluntary act. Voluntariness is a *sine qua non* condition for such assessment, be it positive or negative. A voluntary act is a human act, in the fullest, ethically most meaningful sense of the term. To repeat, for any act to be voluntary, two criteria have to be met: first, the person who performs the act must have sufficient knowledge of all the ramifications of the act; second, the person, in performing the act, must act freely. An act of mine is fully voluntary if I clearly know what I do and I clearly will what I do. Anything that diminishes knowledge of the act, or diminishes the freedom with which the act is performed, in turn diminishes the voluntariness of the act. And with the diminishment of voluntariness, there is diminishment of moral responsibility, hence of the degree of culpability.

Sixteen

Does Ignorance Excuse?

We can be held morally responsible for our acts only if we are fully aware of what we are doing in performing those acts. Common sense tells us as much. Under normal circumstances, we do not blame people, we do not lay upon them the burden of moral guilt when, though they do something damaging, they do not do so deliberately. Accidents happen. At one level of consciousness they knew what they were doing, but at another level they were quite ignorant of the fact that they were doing something damaging, and in most cases we can reasonably assume that, had they known their actions to be damaging actions, they would have refrained from performing them.

Ignorance excuses: that is the basic principle. But it needs to be carefully qualified. Larry was baffled and not a little miffed when he was ceremoniously directed to pull over to the side of the road by a sheriff's deputy in rural Coyote County. He knew for a fact that he had not been speeding. What was it, then, a burned-out taillight or some piddling thing like that? It must be a slow day for the gendarmes if they were out looking for work. Such were Larry's thoughts as the officer of the law approached his car. The deputy politely requested to see Larry's license, gave it quick scrutiny, returned it to him, then asked him if he was aware of the school bus he had passed about a half-mile back. Larry said that he was. Had he noticed that the school bus was stopped? He had. Did he notice that the school bus's red lights were flashing? He did. Then why didn't he stop? "Stop?" Larry queried in return, "why should I stop?" "Because," the deputy patiently explained, "it is state law that all traffic should stop in front of and behind a school bus, in both lanes of a two-lane road, when its red lights are flashing. "But," Larry said, with full confidence, and quite truthfully, "I didn't know that." "Ignorance of the law," the deputy solemnly explained, as he was writing out the ticket, "is no excuse."

Larry got a whopper of a ticket, and I don't think we would be inclined to feel particularly sorry for him. As a licensed driver in his native state, he should have been aware of a law as basic as the one he broke. Larry's ignorance did not excuse, and he fully deserved the ticket the deputy issued to him. Ignorance relieves us of moral responsibility only if it is ignorance for which we ourselves are not responsible. Larry was truly ignorant of the law he broke, but his state of ignorance was due to neglect on his part. He did not know something which he should have known.

Recounting Larry's little run-in with the law offers us the opportunity to call attention to the distinction between vincible and invincible ignorance. Vincible ignorance is the kind Larry displayed; it is ignorance which could and should have been overcome, and for which the ignorant person is therefore responsible. There are any number of things that can bring about vincible ignorance. Often enough it is simply a matter of carelessness on our part, a failure to inform ourselves, and keep ourselves informed, of things that our position and the duties attendant upon it require that we know.

Sometimes we can deliberately keep ourselves in the dark concerning matters about which we should be informed. Willie is steadily dating Wanda, one of the secretaries at the real estate company at which he is one of the crack salesmen. Wanda is both winsome and witty, and they have a lot of fun together. But on a couple of occasions on recent dates she has said things that raised in Willie's mind a disconcerting question: Is this woman married? Though Willie is not exactly a moral paragon, neither is he a man completely devoid of conscience. The codes according to which he was raised would not sanction his keeping company with a married woman, nor, he knew, would his mother, whose opinion he respected. It would not take much for Willie to dispel his ignorance concerning Wanda's marital status. He could simply ask: "Uh, Wanda, pardon me, but do you mind if I ask you a personal question? You wouldn't happen to be married, would you?" Or there are other, more indirect, ways he could find out.

But Willie chooses not to pursue the issue, preserving himself in a state of ignorance. After all, Wanda *is* winsome and witty, and they *are* having such a good time together. The weeks go by, and then one day Willie runs into Pastor Peterson at a local drugstore, who boldly confronts him and censoriously wants to know what Willie thinks he is doing, giving scandal to people by gadding about town with a married woman. Willie feigned shocked surprise. "What, Wanda married? I didn't know that!" Right, Willie, you didn't know that, but you should have known it, and easily could have come to know it. Your ignorance does not excuse.

Sometimes we can be in certain psychosomatic states that prevent us from being properly conscious of what we are doing, and this would have a bearing on the moral evaluation of actions performed in those states. We would not accuse a somnambulist of the deliberate destruction of property if, while sleepwalking through the living room, he knocks over cousin Miriam's priceless heirloom vase and sends it crashing to the parquet floor.

But consider the case of Barney Bixton, who spent the better part of the day in Terry's Tavern, downing one whiskey sour after another. Then, around mid-evening, very unsteady on his feet, he leaves the tavern, climbs clumsily into his car, and heads out in the general direction of his home. He drives only a couple of blocks when he goes through a red light and strikes a teenage boy in a crosswalk, hurling him onto the sidewalk, where he lay unconscious and severely injured. Barney drives on. When the police eventually track him down, a few hours later, he explains to them, in carefully measured but slurred words, and quite sincerely, that he was totally unaware of having run over any pedestrian. Hit and run? Why should he run when he hadn't hit?

Given Barney's state, it was conceivable that he could have struck the boy without being aware of it. He was ignorant of his action because of his inebriated condition. But clearly his ignorance does not excuse. He cannot cite the state he was in to escape moral responsibility for actions performed while in that state, for he was himself responsible for being in the state. Thus, as responsible for the state, he was responsible for the ignorance accompanying it, and for the actions performed in ignorance.

Invincible ignorance is ignorance for which we cannot be held responsible. There are occasions when our actions have deleterious consequences, when we are ignorant of that fact while performing those actions, and— here is the critical point—our ignorance is not something for which we can be reasonably blamed. It cannot be attributable to neglect or carelessness on our part, nor do we bring it about or preserve it by deliberate acts of omission or commission. An episode which we discussed earlier, where Manfred, with a flick of the wrist, ruined an important botanical experiment, could fittingly be judged to be a case of invincible ignorance. No public notice had been given of Dr. Flores's project, and there is no commanding reason why Manfred, given his own position and duties, should have taken any measures to find out about it. Manfred acted in ignorance, but the ignorance was not of his own making.

Recapitulation. Invincible ignorance excuses, vincible ignorance (ignorance that can be overcome) does not. We are not morally culpable for those of our actions which may have damaging consequences so long as (a) we were ignorant of the damaging nature of the actions while performing them, and (b) we cannot be blamed for that ignorance. However, if the ignorance was such that it was under our power to remove, and we did nothing to remove it, we must bear the blame for our ignorant acts.

Seventeen

Can the Will Be Forced?

We have to know what we are doing; we have to will what we are doing. Unless those two conditions are met, our actions are not open to ethical assessment. We really will what we are doing when we act as unencumbered free agents. Once those two conditions above are met, we have a voluntary act, which can also be called a human act. We can give it yet another name: a free act.

If our freedom to act is in any way infringed, our capacity to act as responsible moral agents is accordingly reduced. If we are coerced to do something, or to cooperate in an activity, against our will, our moral responsibility for our actions is directly affected. If the coercion is such that we act in a totally unwilling manner—i.e., we in no way intend the end of the act we perform under compulsion—then our moral responsibility for the act is nil. Only if we act freely can we justifiably be either praised or blamed for our actions.

The most obvious way we can be forced to do something we do not want to do is through physical coercion, as in armed robbery, or rape, or kidnapping. A victim of armed robbery does not want to give what he gives, but the alternative to doing so may be severe bodily harm or possibly even death, so he gives, though unwillingly. The money he turns over to the robber was intended to buy food for his starving wife and children. They must for the time being continue to starve. A most unfortunate situation but, knowing the intention he had for the money which was taken from him against his will, we would not single out the man as a shameful example of a negligent husband and father.

Physical coercion need not necessarily be associated with criminal activity. It can take the form of our finding ourselves in a situation where things are simply beyond our control as far as our ability to act in the way in which we want to act, but the situation may be called "accidental" in the sense that it is not the result of malice or carelessness on the part of anyone.

Gale and Georgia were roommates through their four years of college and became the best of friends. Amidst tearful farewells on graduation day, they made solemn mutual promises that each would attend the other's wedding, come what may. A couple of years later Gale, living in California, got a call from Georgia in St. Paul, announcing her wedding, and wondering if Gale would be there. "Will I be there!" Gale exclaimed. "I promised. Besides, I wouldn't miss it for the world. I'll be there with bells on—wedding bells." Gale purchased her plane ticket well in advance of the wedding, but when she arrived at the airport on the day of her departure she discovered to her agitation that her direct flight had been cancelled. After a frustrating hour of wheeling and dealing, she managed to get a flight to Denver, with the idea that from there she could get a flight to the Twin Cities. But no sooner had her plane set down in Denver when a major winter storm swept in out of the northwest, and within an hour's time all the flights were cancelled. The storm was so severe she ended up spending almost two full days in the Denver airport. She missed her best friend's wedding.

Gale was coerced to do something that was very much against her will—spend two days in Denver, when she wanted to be in St. Paul—but there was no violence involved, no one had deliberately planned to thwart her will in this way. In response to experiences of this sort we sigh, shrug our shoulders, and say things like, "Well, things like that happen. Can't be helped." Georgia was sorely grieved that Gale had missed her wedding, but the thought of blaming her for it never crossed her mind.

Psychological coercion, though more subtle than physical coercion, can be every bit as effective, for it can force people to do what they would otherwise never think of doing, as we saw in the case of Loreen and her experience with the kidnappers. She gave away almost her entire life's savings to criminals, but only because she feared for the life of her daughter. She acted, but she did not act with unqualified freedom. In cases of kidnapping and blackmail, the will is put under direct and oppressive pressure. If the demands made are not met, dire consequences are likely to follow, and it is the fear of those consequences that adversely affects the freedom of the persons being victimized.

The freedom of the will may be curtailed by other forms of influence

which, if not coercive in the strongest sense, can, at least in certain circumstances, be powerfully intrusive. A totalitarian government may set up an
elaborate propaganda machine that seeks to mold and direct the way the
populace thinks, which, if successful, will affect their willed behavior. One
recalls what happened in Nazi Germany. No one is forced to believe propaganda, be it good or bad, least of all if it is so bad that it thrives on outright
lies. But if one is exposed to it for extended periods, and has little or no access to alternative sources of information, it can gradually have a poisoning
effect on the mind and disorient the will. Where there is no free exchange
of opinion, where the truth becomes subject to systematic cynical manipulation, the moral atmosphere of a society becomes polluted, and after a
time citizens are regularly breathing in poison without being fully aware of
the fact.

How are we to think about advertising in this respect? Would it be
going too far to say that it can be psychologically coercive? There is no con-
testing the fact that it influences our behavior. If that were not the case, it
would not be the enormous industry it is. One likes to believe that there is
no devious intent behind it. People's wills are being worked on, there is no
doubt about that, and many and various are the ways in which that is being
done. Through advertising we are either being subtly seduced or directly
urged to buy this, that, or the other thing. There would seem to be no obvious harm in this, so long as what is being bought is really needed. But
how often is that actually the case? "Consumer" is a rather ugly title, suggesting as it does that man's whole reason for being is to devour and digest,
to gobble up as much as he can of the world;s goods over the course of a
lifetime. Consumerism, the mind-set, would seem to be fueled by the delusory conviction that there are no luxuries, only needs. A comparison between the gaudy extravagances of a consumerist society and the economic
condition of most of the world's population raises some pointed questions
having to do with justice.

Our poor wills are under continuous pressure. They are being pushed
and pulled, pelted and pummeled, and put upon in all manner of means.
They are subject to influences which sometimes can be overtly coercive in
one way or another, so that our freedom is thereby infringed upon. We can
be moved to do what we do not really want to do, or prevented from doing
what we very much want to do. For all that, however, our wills, though

prey to a multitude of coercive influences, are, at their core, inviolable. We can be forced to do what we do not want to do, yes, but there is no power on earth that can force us to will what we do not want to will. Therein lies the last, and impregnable, bastion of our freedom.

Eighteen

Is Freedom Possible?

Another name we give to the voluntary act is "free act." Because the moral assessment of an act, in practical terms, comes down to determining whether the act is worthy of either praise or blame, it stands to reason that the act being assessed must be free. It would make no sense to attach praise or blame to an act if it were not done knowingly and willingly, that is, if it were not a free act. In ethics, the buck always stops with the agent, the acting person, who is fittingly praised or blamed for his actions only to the degree that he performs them freely. Without freedom, the moral assessment of human acts is meaningless. Without freedom, there is no ethics; the very idea of morality ceases to be meaningful.

What is freedom? Taken in all its amplitude, it defies precise definition, but then, does freedom really need a precise definition? Some realities are so wide and deep in their substance that any attempt to pin them down in a limited number of words inevitably fails to do them justice. Such is freedom. One of the reasons that we are not particularly bothered by the fact that we cannot precisely define freedom is that we have direct, experiential knowledge of it. We know freedom, not because we can define it, but because we live it.

If we cannot adequately define freedom, we can at least say a few informative things about it. A person can be said to be free, in the most basic sense, if he is not in any way inhibited in his actions. That would be a purely negative understanding of freedom. If I am chained to a stone wall in a dungeon, my freedom of action has been significantly curtailed. I cannot stroll down to the bookstore, or call Uncle Ansgar, or play a game of Scrabble, or engage in any other activities I would prefer to engage in because I am physically constrained from doing so. I have the innate potential to do those things, but that potential is effectively nullified because I cannot exercise it. My freedom is being denied me. Often, we come to have the keenest understanding of what it means to be free when our freedom is taken away from us.

But one does not have to be chained to a stone wall in a dungeon in order to have one's freedom curtailed. Psychological coercion, which trades principally on fear, can prevent us from behaving as we really want to, or can force us to engage in behavior we do not freely choose. Under normal circumstances, people have a right to speak their minds in public, just so long as, in doing so, they do not infringe upon the rights of others. We properly attach special value to the freedom of speech. But the suffocating atmosphere created by a totalitarian society, or totalitarian tactics employed in what is otherwise a reasonably free society, makes people fearful of exercising that freedom, and it is thus curtailed.

We are free when there are no obstacles put in the way of our realizing our potential for action. In more positive terms, we are free because (a) we are the originating source of our actions, and (b) *we ourselves determine the precise form those actions will take.* Freedom is most directly demonstrated in the act of choice. For an act of choice to be such, a choosing person has to be poised before at least two alternatives, A and B, and then himself be the principal determining factor as he opts for either one or the other.

We will put Peter in that situation. There he is, standing before A and B, shifting nervously from one leg to another. He is given the opportunity of choosing between the two. He finally makes his move and chooses A. His choice was free because there was nothing that determined beforehand which of those two alternatives would be his pick—nothing in the stars, nothing in his genes, nothing in his toilet training experiences as a child, nothing in his girlfriend's preferences, nothing Madame Galactia espied in her crystal ball the night before. Mind what I am not saying. I am not saying that those or other things could not have *influenced* Peter's choice. What I am saying is that none of those things *determined* his choice. It was Peter who determined his choice. We might all have taken a guess, before he actually chose, as to whether Peter would pick A or B, and each of us would have had a fifty-fifty chance of guessing correctly, but none of us could have predicted beforehand, with certitude, how the choice would be made. But, for that matter, to a certain extent the same could be said for Peter himself. If he knew beforehand that he was going to point to A rather than to B, then the choice would already have been made, and his pointing to A was simply the public execution of his choice. We know how we are going to choose when we actually choose, when we exercise the volitional act of choice.

There is no determination at work before the choice is actually made because it is the choice itself that does the determining. Peter, by choosing A, exercised his freedom; he made a free choice. That choice is now a matter of history. How can Peter be assured that his choice was in fact free? In order to put it to the test, Peter can ask himself a pointed question: Could it really have been otherwise? He chose A, there is no question about that. But could he have chosen B instead of A? Was there anything forcing him to choose A? Was there anything preventing him from choosing B? If his honest responses to the previous three questions are, respectively, Yes, No, and No, then he has as much assurance as he will ever want that his choice of A was a free choice.

We will now put the choice between A and B in an ethical context. Let B stand for cheating someone, and let A stand for dealing with someone honestly. This time Natasha will be the subject of the thought experiment. She finds herself in a situation whereby, with a little clever legerdemain, she can cheat one of her clients and by doing so stand to make a financial coup of significant proportions. If she opts for B, there is every likelihood that she will soon become a permanent resident of Easy Street. She thinks and thinks about the matter, leans this way, then that way, and then, finally . . . chooses A.

We heave a sign of relief. Good for you, Natasha! Why do we praise people for doing the right thing, and blame them for doing the wrong thing? For one reason only: because we firmly believe that they had a real choice in the matter. People are free to choose to do good, as they are free to do evil, and that is what makes life so pleasant on the one hand, and so dismal on the other. Again, without freedom there would be no ethics, or, ethics would be no more than a diverting word game, like filling in a crossword puzzle for which the answers had already been given. Moral philosophy would be reducible to a purely descriptive sociology.

Since time immemorial there have been philosophers, and others, who have tirelessly dedicated themselves to the task of trying to convince us that we are not really free, that human freedom is no more than a chimera, a delusion. Most people are invariably puzzled when apprised of this point of view. "How can I not be free," the average person would be inclined to wonder, "when I have this persistent, penetrating sense, this steady feeling, this *conviction*, that I am? My freedom is not something I theorize about. It's not the conclusion of an argument. I simply experience it." The philosopher hears this and smiles condescendingly; he clears his throat and speaks: "Ah, well, yes, of course, you *feel* that you are free. We all have that feeling, but, don't you see, that is but an illusion. The fact of the matter is that we really are not free."

So, according to the philosopher, human freedom is but an illusion. (That is the misnomer they commonly employ.) Now, that is an interesting claim. But it is one which, it should be carefully noted, never comes accompanied by anything which, even according to the most generous standards, could qualify as evidence. It is a conclusion that floats in midair, with no premises to support it. In a word, the philosopher has no proof for his assertion that human freedom is an illusion. He simply baldly states it to be the case, and expects to be believed because he holds the H. Dumpty Caldwell Endowed Chair of Higher Psychical and Sociological Studies at Prince Yalvard University.

But what are we to say of the opposing position? Is our freedom, for its part, something that can be proved, in the strict logical understanding of proof? No, it isn't. Should we worry about that? No, we shouldn't. Why not? Because one should not worry about failing to expend energy in attempting to prove the self-evident. The average Joe or Jane on the street has an intuitive awareness of this, and in this respect they are much wiser than the philosopher.

The philosopher's alternative to freedom of the will is strict determinism. This little book is not the proper place to launch into a lengthy disquisition on freedom versus determinism, but I want to make at least one observation. Think of it as a puzzle, which I will leave for you to reflect on at your leisure. If it is true that we are all determined through and through, in every way in which we would care to name, such as, for example, in the way we think, then how is it that some of us are determined to think we are determined and some of us are determined to think that we are not? If everything is in fact determined, then there is no way to decide regarding the truth or falsity of determinism itself. No one is able to free himself from the cage of determinism so that he would be able, from the privileged non-determined perspective which he would then have, to establish whether the cage itself is or is not real.

Nineteen

Rationality

To act ethically is to act rationally. That might surprise some people. In recent years we have been coached to think that ethics has more to do with the heart than with the head, with feeling rather than with thinking. But ethics and logic are not two countries separated by a deep and impassable sea. They are contiguous realms, and traffic should flow freely across their borders, in both directions.

We have already given considerable emphasis to the point that to be ethical is simply to be human in the fullest, the essential sense. A classical definition of man—like so much else, we owe it to the inimitable Aristotle—is "man is a rational animal." Because rationality is the salient mark of our nature as human beings, "becoming human"—the goal of ethics—is tantamount to becoming rational, to living according to the dictates of reason.

Consistently to do what is right and avoid doing what is wrong is not the result of happenstance. It requires thought. We have to use our heads, employ reason, in order to be morally good. To be sure, we can also use our reason to pursue evil, and sometimes with disconcerting effectiveness, but this kind of use is in fact abuse, a betrayal of our nature, for it takes what was intended to serve the good and perverts it by putting it to work in the cause of good's opposite. It would be like using a hammer, a tool intended for constructive purposes, and making it an instrument of destruction.

Just as there are good and bad arguments in political and economic discourse, so there are good and bad arguments in ethical discourse, and it is logic that enables us to distinguish one from the other. It might be helpful if we were at this point to brush up on some elementary logic, by asking two simple questions: What is an argument? What is the difference between a good argument and a bad one?

An argument, in terms of its basic structure, is the soul of simplicity. Every argument is composed of but two parts, premises and a conclusion. No matter how complicated an argument might be in terms of the quantity of its contents, it is analyzable into those two basic parts. (What usually makes arguments complicated is the large number of premises they can contain, and the intricate ways those premises can be interrelated.) Premises relate to conclusion as the supporting to the supported. The conclusion is the statement that the argument wants us to accept as true; the premises represent the evidence that is offered to back up the truth of the conclusion.

> Bobby is an exceptional athlete.
> He won four gold medals in the Olympics.

That is an argument, as simple as they come, because it contains just one premise, and it is stripped of all obvious logical language. In this case the argument leads off with the conclusion, and the premise comes next. We are asked to accept the first statement as true on the basis of the truth of the second statement.

What is the difference between a good argument and a bad argument? A good argument is one whose premises offer sound support for the conclusion. The evidence contained in the premises is convincing; it persuades us to accept the conclusion as true. In that respect the argument about Bobby, just above, is sound. If in fact he won four Olympic gold medals, that represents rather impressive evidence for the claim that he is an exceptional athlete.

Most of the ethically significant choices we make on a daily basis tend to be routine; thus deciding what is the right thing to do in particular situations normally does not require a great deal of reflection. It is when we find ourselves in difficult situations, such as those with which we are not familiar, where easy answers are not readily available, and where careful moral reasoning is called for. But there is at least implicit moral reasoning behind even our routine ethical choices, those that we can make fairly quickly and with confidence because they are the kind of choices we have made many times before. Here there is no need to work through an issue in step-by-step fashion. We have so assimilated certain ethical principles that they are permanent fixtures in our ordinary moral reasoning.

The critical move of ethical reasoning is the application of general principles to particular cases, bringing a rule to bear on *this* act, here and now. Not that this mode of reasoning is unique to ethics. It is employed universally, even in quite commonplace situations. That is how the baseball umpire reasons when he calls a play at second base. The most general of general principles in ethics, that on which all other principles are founded, is: Good is to be done, evil is to be avoided. Nothing could be clearer. And it would be difficult to imagine anyone taking exception to that principle.

But the principle is so general that, just as stated, its practical applicability would pose insurmountable problems. Immediately we have to infer from that most general principle others which are less general and can thus be given practical application. What we need to be specific about in each case is the question of what constitutes the "good to be done" in this or that particular situation. An example: Private property should be respected. Respecting private property is clearly a good, but the principle would be given sharper focus if we were to draw out a specific implication of that principle and say: Stealing is wrong. That statement is refreshingly lacking in ambiguity, and because its meaning would escape none of us, it serves as a clear guide for our behavior. General principles such as "stealing is wrong" serve as the starting points for what is known as the practical syllogism. Using that principle as the starting point—the major premise—the argument goes as follows:

Stealing is wrong.
Surreptitiously removing twenty dollars from
the office coffee fund with the intention of keeping
the money for one's personal use would be an act of stealing.
Therefore, that act must not be done.

The argument begins with a self-evident moral principle. The second premise, or minor premise, is the heart of the argument, for it is the identification of a specific act as representing an instance of what is stated to be wrong in the major premise. The general principle is applied to a particular case. Whether or not the argument is sound turns on the accuracy of the identification made in the minor premise. What makes this an emphatically *practical* argument is its conclusion. It does not simply provide us with information, but gives us a very clear directive.

To repeat, the critical move of moral reasoning is applying general principles to particular cases, and this involves providing sound minor premises
for the practical syllogism. But the major premise, or starting point of the
argument, must also be sound. We might begin a syllogism by describing
stealing as taking what belongs to another without their knowledge or permission. Is that a sound major premise? Does it cover every case we might
imagine? A little reflection would tell us that there can be situations where
peremptorily helping ourselves to the property of others, without their
knowledge or permission, would not necessarily count as stealing. An example: George arrives home late one night to discover his garage is on fire.
He quickly estimates that by the time the volunteer fire department could
arrive on the scene the building would very likely be burned to the ground.
He then remembers that his neighbor, Fred, keeps an industrial-size fire extinguisher in his garage. Fred and his wife are away on vacation. George
rushes over to Fred's garage, breaks in, gets the fire extinguisher, dashes back
to his garage and puts out the fire, with only minor damage having been
done to the building. Should George be accused of stealing? No. As soon
as Fred and his wife returned from their vacation he informed them what
he had done; he subsequently paid for the replenishment of the fire extinguisher, and for the damage he did to Fred's garage when he broke into it.

Twenty
Balanced Life

Extreme behavior, either going too far or not going far enough, is hard on everybody. It might seem that extreme behavior is advantageous for the extremist himself, but such advantages are deceptive, and in any event always short-term; long-term, it is the extremist himself who suffers most from his imbalanced way of behaving. To list too far to port or starboard is to risk eventual swamping. Those who have to put up with extreme behavior on the part of others have no easy time of it, for they continually have to anticipate and make damage-control adjustments to the extremist's next erratic move. Extreme behavior, precisely because it is not under the government of reason, tends to be random, hence unpredictable.

A stable pattern of behavior is what all of us should be striving to establish. A balanced life is ultimately founded upon the balanced act. Every act, as we know, is for the sake of an end, but the quality of the end is critically important. Leslie plans to rob a bank. He executes the plan with consummate skill, not surprisingly, for Leslie is an accomplished robber. The result is that he succeeds in accomplishing his purpose and is now richer by $200,000. He then proceeds to Cancun to celebrate his success. Leslie's act can be deemed to be successful only from a purely practical point of view: it accomplished the end for which it was intended. But we would be loath to identify it as successful from a moral point of view. Without hesitancy we classify it as an unqualifiedly bad act, bad because its end was bad. The morality of an act is importantly determined by the end of the act, what the act is all about.

An imbalanced act is defective either by reason of excess or defect. It contains either too much or too little of what is needed by way of action in order to accomplish something which may be of itself quite worthy of accomplishment. Leslie's act was excessive right from the beginning, in terms of the bad end toward which it was directed; any behavior that is ordered toward achieving an evil end is by that very fact extreme behavior. But we can intend a perfectly respectable goal and yet go about attempting to achieve it in ways which are clearly counter-productive. Doing too much or too little, then, is simply to go about things the wrong way in order achieve a worthy end.

Consider the case of two high school teachers, Marigold and Beverly, both of whom were on the faculty of Hilger High, an institution—to put it kindly—of questionable academic standing, whose students were not especially known for their passion for learning. Discipline was a major and continuing problem at Hilger High. Both Marigold and Beverly acknowledged the importance of discipline in the classroom, and both readily agreed that, without discipline, no effective teaching can take place, and, without effective teaching, there is no learning. So, both saw discipline and learning as effectively coalescing in a single end, an end devoutly to be desired by every good teacher. But they had distinctly different ideas as to how that end was to be achieved.

Marigold was a quiet, demure young lady who had a degree in mathematics, *magna cum laude*, from Berkeley. Her love for mathematics was total, and had something of a mystical tinge to it. She was convinced that once students were brought to see the pristine beauty and commanding rationality of mathematics, they would become, like her, completely enamored of the science and, importantly, it would have a transforming effect on their entire lives. Disciplinary problems, she fondly believed, would pretty much take care of themselves, or, rather, they would be taken care of by mathematics. If the need should ever arise to address disciplinary problems directly, she would do so in a calm, rational manner. She would reason with the students, and they would come to recognize the inherent counterproductive nature of any classroom misbehavior they were engaging in. Punishment should play no part in her pedagogy.

The results of Marigold's approach were not noticeably successful. Even the most earnest of her efforts to communicate to her students the beauties and benefits of mathematics fell on deaf ears, or at least on highly distracted ears, on account of the commotion that was pretty much a constant in her classroom. Her attempts to address disciplinary problems directly, through reasoned dialogue—which she felt pressed to do more and more frequently— were met, on the part of the instigators, with bemused indifference. In the end, and notwithstanding her unquestionable sincerity and good intentions, Marigold failed to establish the kind of discipline in the classroom which is the prerequisite for effective teaching, and her students learned precious little mathematics.

Beverly was an English teacher. She was quite different from Marigold in just about every salient respect. She was a big woman—standing six foot three inches in her stocking feet— blond, bold, and brash. A graduate of Michigan State, she won letters in basketball and track, and in her senior year captained the basketball team. She was still a high school student when she earned the black belt in karate. Beverly's philosophy of discipline in the classroom was very simple: you rule with an iron hand. The teacher is the boss, and from the first day she walks into the classroom she has to establish complete, unqualified control. Even the slightest sign of unruly behavior on the part of any student has to be addressed immediately and forcefully.

Beverly practiced her theory. On one occasion, very early in the semester, a young man in the back row, testing her, started to act up while she was at the blackboard, explaining what was relative about a relative clause. She dropped the chalk on the floor, marched back to the student and told him to stand up. He stood up. Looking up at him—he was a very big kid— she began reading him the riot act, using language that none in the classroom had ever heard fall from the lips of an English teacher. In the midst of this diatribe the student made the mistake of giving her a little shove on the shoulder. The next thing he knew he was on his knees, having his head ground into the mopboard. After a few seconds of this she jerked him to his feet, hip-hopped him to the door, and, just about literally, threw him out of the room. Then she quietly closed the door and returned to the board and there calmly resumed her lesson on relative clauses. The entire class paid rigid attention to what she had to say.

Beverly was not a contributor to grade inflation. The best any student could expect from her, on the themes she had them write on a regular basis, was a "C." In her comments on the students' writing, which were often copious, she could be caustically negative, and was constantly berating them for their linguistic ineptitude. Beverly was satisfied in her own mind that she was a good teacher, and that she maintained the proper kind of atmosphere in the classroom. But what she chose to call discipline was more like a reign of terror. She intimidated all of her students, and positively frightened a fair number of them. And this adversely affected their performance. She had so undermined their confidence in their own abilities, such as they were, that in any given class only a couple of them, three at most, appreciably improved their writing skills, and that was in spite of her influence rather than because of it.

Both Marigold and Beverly were attempting to achieve the same end: to establish a classroom environment in which effective teaching can take place. They both missed the mark, Marigold by undershooting it, Beverly by overshooting it. Marigold failed to appreciate the kind of active, even at times assertive, role a teacher must play in order to maintain discipline in a high school classroom. Beverly, for her part, did not understand that the purpose of discipline is to channel spirits, not break them.

Twenty-One
Attention

Good people, people who live an ethical life, are hard to describe. We know them when we see them, but they are not easy to pin down in precise terms. What is it we detect in them, that prompts us to call them good? What is it that makes them stand out so refreshingly as heartening alternatives to the kind of humdrum, blurred behavior that too many of us are willing to allow ourselves to lapse into? For one thing, in a peculiarly canny sort of way, good people always seem to know what is *really* going on around them, in whatever social environment they might find themselves. They seem seldom to be caught by surprise, even by the most untoward or outlandish events. What it all comes down to, so it seems, is the matter of attention. Attention. Good people are especially noteworthy for their remarkable ability to pay attention.

Attention is one of the mainstays of the ethical life. All of us, I think, would readily acknowledge the general importance of attention. Notice all the play we tend to give to "focus." We earnestly tell ourselves that whatever it is we are involved in, it is imperative to be focused, to keep our eye on the ball, because if we don't, we are surely going to miss it. Being focused, paying attention—two phrases that reflect the same very important state of mind.

Pay attention! That is commonly employed imperative, especially as directed toward children. "Jimmy!" admonishes Miss Marmion, the third-grade teacher, "now you pay attention!" What makes the imperative especially informative is what it tells us about the nature of attention: it *costs* something. Attention demands effort. There is nothing automatic, nothing that we might be prepared to call "natural" about the peculiar state of mind that is being called for. This is especially the case with regard to the kind of attention the ethical life demands of us. That is because the things upon which we need to concentrate are not usually of the type that normally call for our attention. They may in fact be calling, but we are not hearing. If someone sets off a firecracker behind my chair, that is very likely to command my immediate attention. But once the acrid smoke clears and my heartbeat resumes its regular rhythm, I go back to my reading. A big noise can momentarily force full attention, but we quickly withdraw it once we see that the big noise has no interesting intelligible content behind it.

We live in very distracting times. The electronic age has submerged us in a vast, turbulent sea, alive with teeming and often stinging stimuli. The distractions are pervasive and incessant, and if we indiscriminately expose ourselves to them they will keep us in a constant state of tipsy titillation, which is the very antithesis to the kind of state we need to be in if we are to rightly pay attention to things. Attention is a state of consciousness which is directed, selective, sustained, and absorbent. When we are bombarded by sensations, it is very difficult, if not impossible, to direct our attention to something specific and keep it focused there. Often we do not even make the selections; they are made for us. The proof that Albert was really paying attention to X is that, after the experience, he can tell you something intelligent about X, simply by referring to his memory, which duly registered the experience because of his absorbing, sustained consciousness of it. And that happened because he was able in the first place to focus exclusively on X, to selectively separate it from other sensations.

Attentiveness provides the proper psychological ambience within which a mental act takes place, and it is necessary for the success of the act. It is because of *sustained* attention that the act achieves the end toward which it is directed. In working a math problem, the end toward which we are directing our mental activity is the problem's solution. The sustaining of attention until the end of a mental act is successfully achieved is the temporal aspect of attention. But it has an intensity aspect as well. If the math problem we are attempting to solve is a particularly demanding one, you must not only stick with it, but give it extra concentration. You must pay "close" attention to the problem.

There is also a certain defensive aspect of attention, part of the cost which it exacts from us. Because we live in such a distracting world, because so much clamors for our attention which is not worthy of it, we have to work hard at times to beat back all the militant nonsense which is ever threatening to invade our psychic territory. We have to be constantly on the alert. The would-be invaders can sometimes be obnoxiously provocative, and extreme defensive measures may sometimes be called for. Toss out the TV. Extricate yourself from the captivating intricacies of the WWW.

Back to Miss Marmion, the third-grade teacher, who is constantly having to admonish Jimmy to pay attention. It could be the case that her admonishments are uncalled for. Jimmy may very well be paying attention; the problem is, he is not paying attention to what he should be paying attention to. It is one thing to train ourselves to pay attention, but that is only half the task. The other half is paying attention to the right things, the things that are worthy of our attention.

The principal things worthy of our attention, from the point of view of ethics, can be grouped together into three categories: "the self," "the other," and "the transcendent."

Twenty-Two
Attention to Self

Though it might sound odd to modern ears, ethics is properly called a science, for it conforms to the classical understanding of the term. A science, according to the classical definition, is an organized body of thought, based upon first principles, and which seeks to discover the causes of the things it studies. The scientific status of ethics is importantly qualified by its being identified as a practical science, which means that we study ethics not simply to know certain things, but so that we can apply our knowledge to real-life situations. We want to know the nature of justice, for example, so that we will be able to act justly. The knowledge of ethical theory is intended to shape not only our minds but our behavior. (Recall the practical syllogism.) The person who really "knows" ethics is the one who acts ethically, just as the person who "knows" golf is one who plays the game exceptionally well.

Given the practical nature of ethics, its serious study makes special demands of us, for the whole idea is to try to establish a harmonious relationship between ethical principles and the way we conduct our lives. That invariably entails making some significant adjustments to our behavior. Creatures of habit that we are, most of us would prefer to continue to do as we have been doing, following ways with which we are comfortably, perhaps too comfortably, familiar.

Ethics involves reformation, the re-figuration of the patterns of our behavior: thus its practical orientation. Most of us would readily acknowledge the need for the reformation of human behavior, but usually the behavior we have in mind is that of other people. I might be complacently confident that I'm quite okay, but I'm not so sure about the fellow next door. But ethics will not permit that kind of evasive shift of focus. The behavior under consideration must be our own. The self must be the first focus of our attention.

"Know Thyself"— such was the arresting imperative inscribed over the portal of the shrine at Delphi in ancient Greece. The fact that it is an imperative implies that the Greeks of old did not consider genuine self-knowledge to be something we come by naturally, or easily. As rational creatures we are capable of having penetrating knowledge of many and varied things. It does not follow, however, that we are necessarily going to have even adequate knowledge of our own selves. It is not of course that we are in a state of complete ignorance on this score, as if the self were a complete *terra incognita.* We can have knowledge of the self, but it may be unreliable, even perhaps seriously distorted.

But how can we be ignorant about ourselves? When the knowing subject and the object of the knowing are one, can there be any possibility of there being serious obstacles to knowledge? Proximity to an object usually provides considerable advantages to the knowing subject in the effort to gain reliable knowledge of the object. But that does not necessarily hold when it comes to self-knowledge. Here the very proximity and familiarity with the object is what can raise special difficulties; our closeness to the object can blur our vision of it, and familiarity with it does not guarantee reliable knowledge of it. We need to distance ourselves from ourselves, as it were, to gain the perspective to allow us to get a clearer view of ourselves.

The principal explanation for our having a less than clear view of the self is our tendency to think of ourselves in isolationist terms. That is to say, we either miss entirely, or have an imperfect appreciation of, the critical factor of *relation,* of how the self is inseparably related to the other, and how that relation is the key to getting to the deeper regions of the self. To put it differently, we very often do not have sufficient awareness of how the Me is inextricably bound up with the Not-Me, or, to put it in the properly personal terms, with the You.

There is no quicker nor more efficient way to dispel the delusion that self-knowledge is infallible than to compare our own estimate of ourselves with one made by a friend who has our best interests at heart. The mirror we hold up to ourselves has a way of flashing back a flattering image; what we see reflects the pleasantly pretty person we think ourselves to be. But there can be a disconcerting disjunction between what we think ourselves to be and what a friend thinks ourselves to be. Our immediate reaction may be to reject the friend's estimate of ourselves, but if we are wise we will listen and consider carefully. Again, the assumption here, an important one, is that the one who is doing the talking is a true friend, the kind which Aristotle speaks of in his *Ethics*. In the Book of Sirach we read: "A faithful friend is beyond price, no sum can balance his worth."

Ajax is convinced that he is a poet, and an exceptional one at that, one who is destined one day to be numbered among the all-time greats. This is a view, however, which is shared by only his mother and his girlfriend, the opinions of neither of whom can be regarded as being entirely disinterested. Those who are best qualified to make a responsible judgment concerning this matter, the several genuine poets who are acquainted with Ajax and his work, are unanimous and emphatic in the opinion that Ajax, as a poet, is, in fact, severely lacking, and that his condition in this respect would appear to be beyond remedy. Ajax is familiar with the opinion of the genuine poets, but he rejects it out of hand, telling himself that, given the genius that he is, he alone is qualified to estimate his artistic worth.

Our concerns here are limited to what we might call Ajax's artistic self, and therefore to his knowledge of himself specifically as a poet. How can there be any hope of his ever coming to a true knowledge of himself, as a would-be poet, if he is unwilling to accept the opinions of those who are in the best position to enlighten him on that score? He has to shed himself of his delusory self-estimates, and be docilely accepting of learned and sincerely proffered opinions of his worth as poet. The process will undoubtedly be painful, but in the final analysis all will be gain for him by his acknowledging and learning to live with the truth. Ajax's situation is not unlike that in which any one of us could find ourselves with regard to our status, not as poets, but simply as persons.

Rationalization, a process by which we veil ourselves from ourselves, has proven to be one of the most efficient means of self-deception. To rationalize is to reason, but it is to reason in such a way that the proper end of reason, the truth, is not realized. It might be described as lying to oneself, in which there is at work, as is the case with every form of lying, a studied duplicity. We supply ourselves with information concerning the evaluation of our actions and their motivations, which evaluation, we assure ourselves at one level of consciousness, is altogether reliable, but which, at a deeper level, we know to be false. The success of rationalization depends on our ability to mute the voice coming from the deeper level of consciousness.

Know thyself. Is there any systematic and beneficial path we can pursue that will allow us properly to honor that very demanding imperative? If we are looking for a pat formula which, if followed, will gain us the kind of self-knowledge upon which a sound ethical life depends, it is not to be found. But two generalizations might prove helpful.

We need to come to appreciate the critical importance of silence. Internal silence is what is being referred to here. It is critically important. But that cannot be achieved without a certain amount of external silence. We must take measures on a periodic basis to separate ourselves from the ubiquitous din with which our world resounds. The purpose of the silence is to create an atmosphere in which some effective self-questioning can take place. If we lack adequate self-knowledge it is very often because we seldom question ourselves in ways that will serve to peal off the layers of evasion and subterfuge which have been laid on by years of accomplished rationalization on our part. What should the questions be about? Principally, about our motives for doing what we do. The questions must be persistent, pointed, and penetrating, intended to ferret out the deepest motives of our behavior. It can be a rather disturbing business at times, but it has to be done.

We must not imagine that an adequate self-knowledge, vitally important for the ethical life, is something we achieve once and for all. Like so much else having to do with moral reformation, it is an ongoing process. We can never have complete knowledge of ourselves because, in any number of ways, we ourselves are not complete. The self we are attempting to know is a self which is, in a sense, continuously in the making, for better or for worse, and that means we have to maintain a steady pace to keep up with it. Our self-knowledge must be continuously updated.

Twenty-Three

Attention to Others

Though it is scarcely likely to yield a fruitful self-knowledge, there is a kind of attention that we pay to ourselves which comes with effortless ease. It is virtually automatic, and almost as continuous as consciousness itself. In the mind's eye of each of us, we have ourselves prominently positioned at center stage, and very much in the spotlight. This kind of self-awareness, though vivid, is too often quite superficial, and in that particular respect it is similar to the attention that, not uncommonly, we are wont to give to others.

Serious attention to others, which is to say, the kind of attention that touches upon the person, does not come easily. Of course, unless we are unfortunately in a state of unusual insensitivity, we are never completely oblivious to those around us, especially those with whom we associate on a day-to-day basis. But if we were to stop to take a close look at the kind of awareness we all too commonly have of others, we would notice that it has a distinct self-referential quality to it. What Jasper most often most notices about Clotilde, his fiancée, would tell us more about Jasper than it would about Clotilde. In intensely competitive atmospheres, our interest in others might consist chiefly in narrow, self-protective concerns, as we worry over how they might be gaining on us, or rashly intruding on our turf.

It is hard enough to pay the right kind of attention to ourselves—the kind that will eventuate in a productive self-knowledge—but it is much harder to pay the right kind of attention to others, and yet doing so is integral to the ethical life. There is a set order in the proceedings that cannot be violated. Paying the right kind of attention to others can never precede paying the right kind of attention to ourselves. It is naive in the extreme to suppose that we can properly understand others if we don't really understand ourselves.

This is shown in those cases where we adeptly identify, in others, faults which are deeply rooted in ourselves, but which, because of our lack of self-knowledge, we might be completely blind to. The most extreme case of a situation of this sort would be one in which we are simply projecting our own faults onto others, faults which perhaps they really don't have, or at least don't have to the extent that we suppose. To be sure, we could be recognizing what are real faults in others, but often our lack of adequate self-knowledge makes it almost inevitable that we will exaggerate them. Peccadillos are elevated to the level of capital crimes. Thus, our ignorance of self becomes the source of our ignorance of others.

Assuming that we have managed to achieve the proper kind of attention to ourselves, what would a proper attention toward others consist of? It must begin and end with recognizing them as persons, acknowledging each and every "other" as an inviolable *someone*, never as a dispensable something. Personhood necessarily entails uniqueness. All of us share the same nature, human nature; you are a human being, I am a human being. But we do not share personhood. Your personhood is yours and yours alone, and so it is with each and every one of us. As persons, we are unique and unrepeatable. If we are capable of giving due recognition to that crucial fact about one another, then we are paying the right kind of attention to one another. We are properly conscious of personhood, and all it implies.

Personhood is an existential reality; it is simply *there*, to be recognized and acknowledged—or to be ignored. It is not a status which we confer on others. The choice to ignore the personhood of others, or effectively to deny it, expectedly has negative consequences for those who are the victims of that choice. The many and mournful examples of what the poet Wordsworth called "man's inhumanity to man" can all be traced to the denial of personhood. But the denial of personhood is not done without severe cost to the one who is doing the denying. He who denigrates others by failing to recognize them as persons, by that very act denigrates himself. The slave master, by the acts and attitudes by which he depreciates the very humanity of the slave, depreciates his own humanity as well.

What naturally follows upon the acknowledgment of personhood is the unconditional respect for persons, a respect which is grounded on nothing else but the awareness of persons as persons; we are simply responding to a basic reality. No further information is necessary, no additional credentials need be presented. Respect for persons must be elementary, subtending every other kind of response we can have toward others. To have a proper respect for a person need not include liking the person, but it formally precludes the possibility of ever hating him, for the essence of hatred is depersonalization. Liking or not liking others is a subjective thing, and often has its source in temperamental factors over which we have no control. There is no contradiction in saying that we can love a person without particularly liking him.

We are told to love our neighbor. The philosopher Simone Weil began to wonder seriously about that injunction. Why should we love our neighbor? What is it about him that should make it imperative that we love him? Weil's provocative response to the question was this—simply the presence of her neighbor. We should love our neighbor simply because he is present to us. He exists. That attitude beautifully expresses an unconditional acknowledgment of personhood.

Twenty-Four
Attention to Transcendence

A purely naturalistic ethics would be one that interprets human behavior in exclusively human terms. A purely supernaturalistic ethics would be one which fails to give the human element its proper due. The ethics which I am sketching in this book, which I call a fully human ethics, is one which, while focusing its attention on the human, sees the human as subsumed within a larger reality, the relation to which lends to the human complete intelligibility precisely as human. It is an ethics which not only acknowledges the reality of the transcendent— i.e., that which is beyond, and superior to, the human—but regards it as something that philosophy cannot afford to ignore.

We are incorrigibly comparative thinkers, and seldom, in our comparison of any two things, if we look at them closely, do we find them exactly the same. There is always some nuance of difference between them that we are able to detect. The difference might be precisely quantified—one thing weighs 3.2 grams more than the other—or it may not lend itself to that kind of precise differentiation, and we have to settle for phrases like "better than," or "more beautiful than."

Freddie, faced with the momentous decision of having to choose between two shiny red Fuji apples to serve as a mid-afternoon snack, discovers, upon close inspection, that one of the apples is blemished by a bruise. That makes the two apples, in that particular respect, different. And it also makes the unbruised apple, for Freddie, the better one, and that apple becomes the fare for his snack.

Good, better, best—those are the three pivotal terms by which we give a general framework to our comparative ways of thinking. Of the three terms, "best" turns out to be the most potentially revealing of the deepest ontological truths. When we employ those terms we are doing two things: first, and very basically, we are showing a positive response to an object to which we apply them; second, we are acknowledging that there are degrees of goodness. There is the good, the better, and the best. However, those three very broad terms do not exhaust the degrees of goodness that we discover in the objects of our love and desire. In some cases a particular kind of good might be so various in its instantiations that the degrees of goodness it displays are beyond counting, and what we are confronted with is a complex hierarchy of goodness. And resting at the top of every hierarchy, scintillant in its uniqueness, is "the best."

What do we mean by the best? If we attempt to deal with the idea in a purely abstract manner, the most we can do, by way of explaining it, is to offer synonyms for it. We end up saying things like, "Well, the best is the supreme, the maximum, the apex, the pinnacle, the prime, the greatest, the optimum, the paramount, the unparalleled, the matchless, the peerless, the superlative, the utmost, the highest . . . ." I won't go on. That purely linguistic approach is helpful only to a limited degree. The most productive way to get a sure grasp on what the idea of the best is attempting to disclose to us is to apply it to particular objects, which, as a matter of fact, is what we habitually do. "That was the best football game I've seen in my life." "This is the best essay submitted to the contest." "Beth is simply the best."

If we want to understand the best, we have to think in concrete terms and start by asking, The best *what*? We may consider something as simple and unpretentious as apples. Because apples constitute a very large category, given the various kinds of apples there are, we will shrink the category and consider only Fuji apples. In comparing any two Fuji apples, as Freddie was doing earlier, we can without too much difficulty, using whatever criteria we choose, designate one as being better than the other. But the matter becomes more challenging if we were to be presented with a whole bushel basket full of Fuji apples, and are asked to choose the single best one among them. We agree to do this. After lengthy inspection, re-inspection, and cogitation, we eventually come up with what we consider to be the best Fuji of the batch.

Granting the possibility of being able to select the best apple among a bushel basket full of them, does it make any sense to speak of *the* best Fuji apple, that is, a Fuji apple that is superior to any other Fuji apple now existing, or which ever has existed? Let us imagine that there is such a Fuji apple, and here it is right before us on the table, in all its lustrous, incontestable superiority. But how was the selection of the supreme Fuji apple made? It was by a reference to what those who made the selection conceived to be the ideal Fuji apple, their conception of the most complete, perfect way to be for this particular kind of being—a Fuji apple. The ideal Fuji apple transcends all individual Fuji apples and exercises a governing influence over them by the fact that it is the permanent standard by which all of them are evaluated.

Whether we are dealing with apples or oranges, or whatever it is we come to designate as "the best," it is the ideal we appeal to in doing so—the ideal football game, the ideal essay, the ideal person. Whenever we are faced with any object we are moved to evaluate, the mind naturally soars to the heights, imagining a supreme way of existing for that object, the ideal, and that becomes the guiding criterion for the evaluation.

The ideal exercises a commanding presence in ethics. In the ethical choices we make, as we pursue the goods we believe will be perfective of us, it is always the ideal of the best that drives us on, an ideal that we can justifiably call transcendent, because it always seems to surpass every concrete instance of what we choose to call the best. And that explains why we are never completely satisfied with whatever good we might come to possess, however good it might in fact be: we see that it does not quite measure up to the ideal. The transcendence of the ideal is attested to by the fact that it endures through any number of specific applications. My enthusiastic avowal, "That was the best football game I've seen in my life," does dispense with the ideal, for if I see a game next season that I judge to be better than my previous "best," it is an appeal to the ideal that allows me to make that comparative judgment.

The best, the ultimate, the final end, happiness, the supreme good—they are all different ways of saying what amounts to the same thing. It is what we all want, what we cannot help but want. It haunts us. I have called the best an ideal. Does that mean it is not real? What might we cite as a sure mark of anything that we are inclined to call "real"? Is it not its capacity to move us, to get us to act, to behave rationally, i.e., with the idea of achieving an end which we see as perfective of us? The supreme good moves us in precisely that way. Every limited good that we pursue, however trivial it might be, has enfolded within it a hint, however faint, of the limitless good.

Take any actually existing thing, a real object, that you are prompted to call "the best." Assume that your judgment is astute and highly informed, and that the object itself is very impressive. What is implied by your judgment is that the object represents the supreme way of existing, for the kind of object it is. And that, in turn, implies that there are tiered ways of existing, that there are degrees of being, that some things are more declaratory in their sheer presence, more fully and emphatically in place existentially, than are other things. Granting that, something most significant is being suggested to us. Because we regularly recognize, in real objects of which we have direct knowledge and which we call "the best," because we see a supreme way of existing in them (for the kinds of things they are), might it not be that, in the realm of being itself—taking into account all that possibly exists—there is a "best" without qualification, a "best" pure and simple, the ultimate in terms of real existence, a maximum way of being which transcends all the beings we know and which accounts for their being just what they are? Such a being would be the Supreme Being.

Twenty-Five
We Cannot Go It Alone

A sure sign that we have not fully succeeded in the matter of self-knowledge would be indicated by the ability to hold in our minds, with no discomfiture, two incompatible propositions: (1) "I know myself"; (2) "When it comes to the ethical life, I can go it alone." If Xavier sincerely believes what is expressed in the second proposition, then the first is false. Xavier does not know himself, for if he did he would be keenly aware of the fact that the kind of rugged individualism reflected by the second proposition does not sit well with the ethical life. If self-knowledge is genuine, it knows that the self is heavily dependent on others. Being ethical necessarily involves togetherness, community.

Aristotle regarded personal ethics and social ethics, or politics, as two sides to the same thing; this is not a surprising view for a philosopher who famously defined man as a political animal, which is to say, a creature whose natural environment is social. Other philosophers, by way of contrast, have imagined a primitive state of nature where all the members of the human species were by nature rugged individualists. According to one scenario, in this state of nature men carried on continual warfare with one another, a brutal and ceaseless conflict where they behaved as wolves. Eventually, become weary of constant contention, and possibly realizing that the current modus vivendi sharply diminished the prospects for personal survival, our primitive ancestors sat down and signed a mutual non-aggression pact; peace was established and the way was made clear for political organization. In line with this theory, man is not social by nature but at one point in his primitive history decides to opt for socialization as a matter of expediency, to make for a more predictable, less dangerous environment. Aristotle would have considered a putative pre-social state of the race to be pure fiction. Man the political animal did not evolve from man the individualist; rather, the individualist is a corruption of man the political animal.

Individualism is what happens when man attempts to repudiate his proper nature.

One of the signs of a mature moral consciousness is the prominence in it of the idea of the common good. The term is a familiar one, often spoken, but there is little clarity today in the ideas behind it. A common misunderstanding of the common good is to regard it as an aggregate of sorts, the sum total of all individual or private goods. A common good, as the term itself makes explicit, is a good that belongs to many, and that is precisely what a private good, by definition, is not and cannot be. You can add up as many purely private or individual goods as you like, but that will never give you the common good. A common good is communal, and as such is equally shared by all individuals who belong to a community of whatever kind; however, the term is most often used as referring to a political community or state.

Examples of specific common goods encompassed within the general common good would be all the basic human rights, such as those cited in the Jeffersonian triad of life, liberty, and the pursuit of happiness. Liberty or political freedom is a good which is shared by all members of a healthy political community, and which benefits all. It has both a negative and a positive side to it: freedom *from*, and freedom *for*. The citizens of a well-regulated political community are free from being subjected to physical violence to their own persons, free from unjust laws, free from public conditions that would force them to violate their consciences, and free from any number of untoward things that they would have to contend with were they to live in a seriously disordered civil society, one without a general common good. On the positive side, citizens are free to own and dispose of property as they see fit, free to assemble with other members of the community, free to speak the truth in public, and free to participate actively in their own civil governance.

If the individual goods that we pursue are real goods—i.e., goods that are really beneficial for us—and if we live in a political community where the common good is in a healthy condition, then there should be no tension between the two. In fact, it is precisely a healthy common good, one in which all the natural human rights are duly honored, that serves to protect individual goods, creating an atmosphere in which legitimate individual goods can be pursued without restraint or inhibition. Indeed, the healthiest kind of common good can be said actively to foster the pursuit of legitimate individual goods, by the favorable social climate it creates and sustains. On the other hand, an unhealthy common good puts private goods in jeopardy. Living as he does in a society that prohibits private property, Joel's dream of one day owning a little patch of land in the country where he can grow beets and write poetry must, until the political situation changes for the better, remain a mere velleity.

To have a lively awareness of the common good and its critical importance for our lives is to be aware of the fact that our own personal well-being can never be something which is cut off from the general well-being of the society in which we live. There can be no egocentric doing it "my way" that ignores or intrudes upon the legitimate ways of all the others in the community. Moreover, we need the help of others, not simply in order physically to survive, but to lead ethical lives. We might be able to manage sheer physical survival on our own, but not an ethical life, not, that is, a truly human life.

The ideal common good would be one that preserves and protects and fosters what is genuinely humanizing for all the members of the community it embraces. A society that suppresses the free exercise of religion, for example, as many societies have done and continue to do, would thereby be diminishing the humanity of the entire citizenry, for when any one legitimate human freedom is denied, all the others are put at risk and, as actually often happens, they are themselves eventually made subject to curtailment. Atheists living in a society that denies freedom of religion should not be without worry, for, in the thinking of the social engineer, the exercise of any freedom is a gift of the state, and if the state sees fit to deny today the free expression of belief, there is no logical impediment to its denying the free expression of unbelief tomorrow. Freedom is all of a piece.

Each of us is responsible for the maintenance of a healthy common good. We can only effectively do that by thinking inclusively, by keeping in mind the good of others. The various individual goods I pursue will always have, unavoidably, a peculiarly private stamp to them, but they should never be so exclusively private that they are radically incompatible with a healthy common good, nor should there be a clash between my pursuit of legitimate individual goods and my neighbors' pursuit of legitimate individual goods. The common good is not self-creating; it has to be brought into being, put in place, then kept in place, by the members of a political community. We might be by nature political animals, but we are not by nature political animals whose political communities are necessarily characterized by a healthy common good. How is a healthy common good put in place and then kept in place? In more cases than not, by indirection: a society has a healthy common good because it has a critical mass of citizens who consistently pursue real goods, goods that are perfective of them as human beings. It comes down to a rather simple matter: a good society is made up of good people.

A healthy common good creates the right kind of environment for living the ethical life. A more immediate kind of assistance to living that life is provided to us by friendship, as noted earlier. We frequently identify people as friends because we benefit by our association with them in one way or another, perhaps only in a material way. That would not represent the highest kind of friendship, and yet it is nonetheless deserving of the name because it involves no cynical manipulation on the part of those forming the relationship, no "using" of the other; the benefits flow both ways. But because the friendship depends entirely on the benefits that are derived from it, once those benefits cease, so does the friendship. In contrast to friendship of this type, there is what we call simply true friendship.

What chiefly characterizes true friendship is what is put into it, not what is gotten out of it. The friend comes first, as person, not as benefactor. Sarah and Clare are true friends, which means that Sarah puts Clare before Sarah, and Clare puts Sarah before Clare. They are capable of true friendship in the first place because each of them, as individuals, is dedicated to the pursuit of real goods; each lives an ethical life. Because each of them wants only what is truly good for herself, each wants only what is truly good for the other. Because Sarah knows what is truly good for herself, what genuinely would benefit herself as a person, she would not be capable of wishing anything else than what is truly good for Clare. But she does not simply wish this; she *wills* it, which means that she acts upon it. The essence of love is to will what is truly good for the other. The attitude that Sarah has toward Clare is nicely matched by Clare's attitude toward Sarah. In true friendship, there is perfect reciprocity.

Twenty-Six

Further Reflections on the Good

We saw earlier how it is that the notions of end, happiness, and good all coalesce and merge into one. We do whatever we do for the sake of achieving a definite end, which is just another way of saying that we act purposefully. Our purposes motivate us in the forceful way they do because we believe we will be better off for their being realized: achieved purposes will contribute to our happiness. And the good? We believe that the only things that can meaningfully contribute to our happiness are good things. And "contributing to our happiness," we came to see, mindful of the Aristotelian understanding of happiness, amounted to the same thing as increasing our capacity to act virtuously.

The good is the governing idea in ethics, for it is our conception of what we deem to be good which is the motivation behind all of our actions. To see something as good is, in the first instance, simply to regard it in a positive light; at a more reflective level of consciousness we see it as potentially beneficial for us, and that is the triggering factor that puts us in pursuit of it. Of course, what we identify as bad also affects our behavior, but negatively. We turn our backs on what we perceive to be bad, take whatever measures are needed to distance ourselves from it. For a person to evaluate something as bad and then desire it would be to act contrary to the way we are naturally constituted. A truly bad thing has to be converted into a good thing by us before we will take pains to possess it.

While the perception of a good commonly engenders the desire to possess it, there are any number of things we regard as good where there is never any question of our ever coming into possession of them, at least not in the ordinary way we think of possession. I have in mind those things that have a way of capturing and holding our attention in a very special way because they are beautiful—a stunning sunset, a full moon floating above the Eastern horizon, Mozart's Piano Sonata in A major, Vermeer's

"Girl with a Pearl Earring." The experience of beauty, the manner in which we react to it, has the effect, if we reflect on the matter, of expanding our understanding of the nature of the good. Philosophy has long thought of goodness and beauty and truth as different aspects of what is essentially one reality, something like the three sides of a perfect equilateral triangle. Or we might say that beauty is the poetic expression of the good; it is the good as suggestive of the transcendent. When we are face-to-face with beauty, be it natural beauty or the beauty of art, we are encountering something which calls attention to itself in an especially arresting way. And yet, while emphatically calling focused attention to itself, it at one and the same time is pointing beyond itself, to a transcendent beauty, to a transcendent good. By a transcendent beauty I mean a beauty that explains the beauty we see in things; by a transcendent good I mean the good that explains the good we see in things.

What is the explanation, the ultimate explanation, for our identifying anything as good? It certainly will not do to say that it is simply our positive response to something that makes it good, as if "this is good" were to amount to no more than "because I like it." If we are seeing and thinking clearly, it is just the other way around: we favor something, love it, because we are responding to *it* precisely as good. Goodness, then, cannot be reduced to something merely subjective; it enjoys objective status in reality. Because that is the case, there must be an objective explanation for the objective goodness we see and love in the things all around us. Furthermore, it must be an ultimate explanation, in that it is an explanation which does not itself need to be explained, otherwise we will never arrive at a satisfactory answer to our question. Philosophy argues that the only adequate explanation for the goodness of particular things is the existence of an Ultimate or Supreme Good, a complete and unqualifiedly good, in which all particular instances of goodness have their generative source; their goodness is what it is because it participates in the goodness of the Supreme Good.

Further reflection on the idea of the good invariably leads to the matter of evil. Though nothing could be more radically opposite than good and evil, the two are closely related in a very significant way. Goodness is the foundational reality, and evil is existentially totally dependent on it; if there were no goodness, there could be no evil. Evil exists parasitically in relation to goodness. This being true, in attempting to understand the nature of evil, we can only approach it through the good. The good comes first, as the complete, as presence, and the complete presence necessarily precedes the incomplete and absence. St. Augustine classically defined evil as *privatio boni*, the absence of good. The very idea of "absence" depends, for its intelligibility, on the idea of "presence." To put the principle in more basic terms: we can only understand the negative in terms of the positive. Without positive numbers, there are no negative numbers. The good is the positive, evil is the negative. The point being stressed is that we can understand evil, insofar as we can understand it at all, only through the good, and that is because of how it relates to the good: as absence to presence.

Evil just as such is unintelligible, and that is because, just as such, it does not exist as an independent reality. It has no substantial being, but exists as a corrupting feature of substantial being. Like a physical disease, it can be identified only by reference to the living body on which it preys.

It is difficult to try to talk intelligently about evil. Our words become halting and hesitant, and are interrupted by many pauses. And even if we manage to sustain the conversation for some length of time, more words seldom mean more light. Why is this? It has very much to do with the fact that when we talk about good we are talking about *something*, whereas with evil we are trying to grapple with the lack of something. We are trying to put our finger on an absence, something that should be there, but isn't.

Twenty-Seven

The Proper Pursuit of the Good

"Pursuing the good." It is a time-honored phrase, pregnant with provocative implications, and it very nicely sums up the activity constituting the essence of the ethical life. The good is the end our actions are intended to achieve, the goal they are aimed at. We can think abstractly about the nature of the good but, during the normal course of events, we do not pursue abstractions. We go after concrete goods, real things that are really desirable. Ethics, remember, is a preeminently practical science.

When we consider the good as an end, which we naturally do, this immediately suggests means, for wherever there is an end there must be means. Often we do not have to give all that much thought to means, for they can be so simple and undemanding that we take them on with little reflection. There is right now a full pot of fresh coffee out in the kitchen. If the end I have in mind is to have a cup of coffee, the means to be taken to achieve that end will not involve undue hardship. There is usually a close correlation between the importance of an end and the complexity and difficulty of the means required to achieve it. Taking the means required to get a cup of coffee is an effortless task in comparison to taking those needed to, say, get a medical degree.

The test of how serious we are about pursuing a particular end is shown by how willing we are to take the means necessary to achieve it. In some instances we do not know how complicated and difficult means can be until we are actually taking them. Certain tasks, before we launch into them, might seem manageable without the expenditure of too much time and effort, but then they turn out to be more than we had bargained for. And there are always those pesky "unforeseen circumstances" that invariably complicate matters for us. But if we can say to ourselves before we begin the pursuit of a particular goal, "I'll do whatever it takes to get there," and mean it, chances are very good that we will not be diverted by any unexpected difficulties we might meet with along the way.

The means must be adequate to the end. That holds true in two ways. First, and very basically, they must be efficient; they must actually be able to get us to the end for which they are intended. Second, and this applies specifically to ethics, they must be morally acceptable. Let us consider each in turn.

The house that Lucille recently bought was pleasant enough in many ways, but the backyard was a perfect horror. Lucille was a dedicated gardener, however, and she was determined to get things in shape, and in a hurry. There was an area next to the garage that she wanted to make into a vegetable garden, but in its present state it was a jungle of shrubs, saplings, and a variety of other vigorous, out-of-control, ugly, and not readily identifiable flora. To clear the area, Lucille decided to use dynamite, setting it off from a safe distance in front of the house. The means Lucille chose proved to be wonderfully efficient: the area was completely cleared. Unfortunately, Lucille now had a large crater in her backyard, and her garage was gone. To make matters worse, the lady next door had a heart attack when she heard the explosion. All in all, I do not think we are being careless in concluding that Lucille chose inappropriate means to achieve the end of creating the proper conditions for a vegetable garden.

Sometimes there is but a single means available for attaining a particular end. If there is only one road leading from Lost Canyon to Gary's Gulch, and you, who are right now lunching on a buffalo burger at Ye Olde Saloon in Lost Canyon, want to drive to Gary's Gulch, your choice of means to get there is an easy one. More precisely, you have no real choice at all. You either take County Road 3.14 to Gary's Gulch or you never get there, unless you want to walk. In more cases than not, however, there are multiple means that can be taken to achieve the ends we set for ourselves, and that is where we have to put on our thinking caps and try to reckon the best means possible.

Among the things we need to consider in doing so, efficiency should loom large. It goes without saying that it would be an exercise in futility to attempt to achieve an end by relying on obviously inadequate means. Attempting to empty a swimming pool with a teaspoon and bucket would not be an especially efficient way of going about it. But means, to be adequate, must achieve their end in more than a rawly efficient way. The means Lucille chose to get her vegetable garden were efficient, in a manner of speaking, but the collateral damage she caused in clearing the designated area rendered her accomplishment a highly dubious one. Considered ethical judgments are called for in cases of that sort.

In choices that have clear moral implications, we definitely have to take into account more than mere efficiency when we determine the means to be taken to achieve certain ends. First of all, we have to have an eye to the end itself. It must be morally permissible, which is to say that it must be an objectively good end. If Roscoe's purpose is to murder Theodore, he is going to do evil regardless of the means he chooses to achieve that purpose, because the end itself is evil. However, a morally good end can be spoiled by attempting to achieve it by immoral means. The end does not justify the means, as the venerable principle rightly reminds us.

That principle assumes that the end in question is a good one. The idea behind saying that the end does not "justify" the means is that we cannot use any means whatever, no matter how efficient they might prove to be, in order to bring about an intended good end. Clem is a big-hearted guy, and nourishes a deep and genuine sympathy for the poor of the world. When he heard about the family on the east side of town that was in such desperate straits the children were suffering from severe malnutrition, he decided that he was going to do something about it. And he did. He gathered together ten thousand dollars in cash, put it in a plastic bag, and late one warm summer night, went over to the destitute family's house and, St. Nicholas-like, surreptitiously slipped it through an open window. Clem had seemingly done a good deed. But there was a problem. The ten thousand dollars he gave to the destitute family did not belong to him, for he had stolen it that afternoon from the Farmers and Steamfitters State Bank on Main Street. The means he chose to achieve a good end poisoned it, and cancelled for him the positive moral value in what otherwise would have been a commendably virtuous act.

Twenty-Eight
Priorities

"Getting one's priorities straight," or variations thereof, is a phrase that one hears bandied about fairly frequently these days. It can be fruitfully reflected upon. To have one's priorities straight is universally regarded as a good thing. What it means, presumably, is that one has one's priorities (e.g., commitments and intentions) in proper order; they are so stacked up that the most important one comes first, then the second most important, then the third, and so on. This implies that each priority has a certain intrinsic value, and thus it would be its respective value which determines where it would be placed in relation to the others. Let A, B, and C represent various priorities, and let them all belong to Charlie. Let A have a value which is superior to B, and B a value which is superior to C. In order that these priorities be tended to in a "straight" manner, then, they would have to be arranged A, B, C. But bad-luck Charlie attaches most importance to C, lesser to B, and the least to A. So, with respect to A and C at least, he has things completely backwards.

Endowing those skeletal letters with flesh and blood, we will say that A stands for "providing for one's family," B for "being a conscientious citizen," and C for "being a scratch golfer." Charlie, a married man with six children, does quite well with B. He never misses the opportunity to vote, is a member of the Neighborhood Action Committee, and doesn't cheat on his taxes. But what receives most of Charlie's time, attention, and energies is golf. He is monomaniacally devoted to the game, and because he lives in a part of the country where he is able to play it the year around, that is just what he does, with a passion, spending almost all of his free time on the links. However, the time and attention Charlie gives to golf is time and attention taken away from his family. The fact is, he neglects them shamelessly. Because of the relative importance of playing golf, which comes first in his life, as compared to caring properly for his family, which rates a poor third for him, most people would say that Charlie does not have his priorities straight.

They would say that about Charlie, and be right about it, because they recognize that there are certain objective standards according to which priorities can be said to be either properly or improperly ordered. We do not suppose that a set of priorities are properly ordered simply because they suit the personal proclivities of the one who does the ordering. We wouldn't say, "It's Charlie's business how he lives his life," if that is intended to mean that it is no concern to anyone but Charlie alone what behavior he chooses to engage in. (Tell that to his wife and kids.) If Charlie is seriously concerned with living an ethical life, he should be attaching more importance to things that, objectively considered, *are* more important. Playing golf is good, so is properly caring for one's family, but the two goods do not weigh the same. Let Charlie, when he's out on the golf course, give his all to the game, but do so as a dedicated, conscientious family man.

Our hearts are where our treasures are. Our priorities are our treasures, the things that we put first in our lives, that command most of our attention, that we can be said to live for, and some of which can be so important for us, have so powerful a grip on our affections, that we are willing to die for them. Every once in a while we should pause and ask ourselves, seriously: What is the most important thing in my life? Let us imagine that, just a moment ago, every adult human being now living on the face of the earth did in fact pause and ask that question, and gave it an honest answer. Those answers would of course be richly varied, but this much can be said with certainty, that each answer would be deeply revealing of the person who gave it. We identify ourselves by our priorities, by the things we call good, the things in the pursuit of which we shape the very contours of our lives.

To have one's priorities straight in the most significant ethical sense means to have real goods as priorities, things the pursuit of which will redound to our genuine benefit in that they will be perfective of us as persons. We put first things first.

Twenty-Nine
Mistaking the Good

We always choose the good, pursue the good. Always. There are no exceptions to that. If that does not seem quite right to you it is because the claim, though quite true, needs to be importantly qualified. And here is the important qualification: We always choose and pursue what we *perceive* as the good. We cannot do otherwise, try as we might. We simply are unable to desire and then attempt to come into the possession of something which we do not regard as good. An astute observer, taking note of the kinds of choices I all too regularly make, may shake his head in dismay, for he sees that my perceptions leave much to be desired. What I take to be good things are not always so. In other words, I am often sadly mistaken in my judgments regarding the good.

More than once in the preceding pages of this work I have made the distinction between real goods and apparent goods, without pausing to explain that distinction. It is now time to pause and explain it. A real good is one which will be actually perfective of the person who pursues it. When Stephanie promptly pays back to Cynthia the five hundred dollars she borrowed from her, she has done something which is really good, for it represents an act of justice, and those who act justly toward others, better themselves as persons by doing so. An apparent good is one which, though it *seems* that it will be perfective of the person pursuing it, in fact will not be.

Liam, in making out the formal application for the excellent job which he eventually landed, put down any number of rather ripe lies about himself and his past work experience. His lying may have brought him purely material gain in the short term, but we can reliably predict that, in the long term, Liam's lying ways are inevitably going to catch up with him. But the point of the sad story is this: had not Liam seen lying as a good—as something which he believed would accrue to his benefit—he would have had no motivation for doing it. We could appropriately describe Liam's behavior as self-destructive, but self-destructive behavior, even of the most extreme form, is always given a positive twist by those who engage in it. The suicide can only go through with terminating his life because, in his benighted way, he sees his death as a good, as something which is preferable to his continuing to live.

The distinction between real and apparent goods calls to our attention the very obvious but insufficiently appreciated fact that we can be mistaken about the good, something at which we can be depressingly proficient. We all too often see and pursue ends as positive which in fact are negative. What we *perceive* to be the case—that something will be beneficial for us— is not the case. Some of the consequences of our bad choices can be relatively trivial, some quite grave, depending on the nature of the choices themselves. When Bernie tossed back those two extra martinis, it seemed the right thing to do at the time, but the following morning, his head throbbing, he overturned the judgment he had made the night before. When David joined the Foreign Legion, because it seemed to be the only reasonable response to Diane's cruel refusal of his hand, he had five long, sweaty, dust-encrusted years to rue his decision. And what did Diane care?

We all make mistakes regarding the good. An ethical life has as one of its principal aims fostering the effort to keep those mistakes as occasional as we can, preventing them from becoming habitual. The difference between the occasional and the habitual is the difference between virtue and vice.

How is it that we get it wrong about what is truly good for us? In considering particular cases, the explanations can of course, in their details, vary widely, but there are two basic factors which, in one way or another, figure in just about every case, and they are ignorance and emotion. We can be mistaken about the good simply because we do not know enough, about ourselves, about all the salient aspects of the circumstances in which we find ourselves when we make our choices, and this can have a direct bearing on the quality of those choices. Ignorance of oneself, i.e., lack of sufficient self-knowledge, is one of the most common causes for our mistaking apparent goods for real ones, and unless that seminal problem is addressed, the chances of a person's ever being able consistently to get it right regarding the good are very slim indeed. The applicable logic here is disarmingly simple: someone who does not really know himself cannot be expected to know what is truly good for himself.

A mistake about the good caused by the circumstances in which we make our choices may be owing simply to a lack of experience on our part, in which case perhaps the only remedy is more time, time in which more of the right kinds of experience can be accumulated. We learn from our experiences only if we live through them alertly. There is no mistake from which we should be able to learn more than the mistake we make when we opt for an apparent good over a real one. Being stung is not the kind of experience we are inclined easily to forget; it leaves its mark. The single, the infallible, cure for ignorance is knowledge. And the kind of knowledge we need in order to distinguish real goods from apparent ones is gained only through persistent, assiduous effort.

Emotion is another factor that explains why we make mistakes concerning the good. Discerning the real good is an act of reason. It is an eminently rational mode of behavior to pursue those things which will enhance us as human beings; it is simply the intelligent thing to do. We need clear and calm thinking, then, to enable us to choose real goods over apparent ones, especially if what is in question is of great moment. But when it comes to the disruption of clear and calm thinking, few things are more wonderfully effective than runaway emotion. If we allow them to be, our emotions can be imperiously pushy, in which case our mental powers are for all practical purposes neutralized. What was it that made the above-mentioned David so susceptible to the cynical blandishments of the Foreign Legion recruiting sergeant but the emotion of despair over Diane's refusal of him, which had taken so firm a grip on his soul. Any emotion, if strong and dominating enough, muddles the mind. Fear or anger can be so controlling of us that our perceptions of what constitutes the good are completely out of focus, and we end up taking the fake for the authentic.

Though not as pervasive in its influence as ignorance and emotion, another explanation for our mistaking the good is precipitousness—jumping the gun. Sometimes we are so anxious to get on with things that we do not give adequate consideration to what it will take to make things turn out successfully. It would not hurt at times to give heed to the most ancient bits of practical advice: look before you leap; haste makes waste. Patience, patience. No time given to a careful consideration of the good can be counted as misspent.

Thirty

The Breakdown between Knowing and Doing

Socrates had a theory about ethics, a theory that seems to have been adopted by his disciple Plato, which can be expressed succinctly in the following terms: to know the good is to do the good. According to this understanding of it, there is nothing terribly complicated about the ethical life. If I really know the good, know what is the right thing to do in this or that particular situation, I will do it. For Socrates, knowledge was paramount in ethics for its power to effect action—right knowledge guarantees right action—and this led him to equate knowledge with virtue.

It is an interesting theory, and it has to be granted that it greatly simplifies the science of ethics. If I am serious about leading an ethical life, I know exactly what I have to do: study and learn, master the lore. Then I will live according to the lore. My actions will perfectly reflect my knowledge. Specifically, once I know what the virtue of justice is all about, I will be a just man.

The Socratic theory provides us with a ready-to-hand explanation for why people behave badly: they don't know any better. Their problem is that they are ignorant of the good. If they knew the good, they could not help but do it. Carrie is carrying on in a manner that makes us all blush for her: plagiarizing shamelessly, brutalizing her subordinates, bad-mouthing her friends, neglecting her mother, smoking with impunity in no-smoking zones. This is all very sad, of course, but it is not Carrie's fault, you see. She does not really want to do evil, but given the unbreakable link between knowledge and action, she has no choice but to act according to what she knows. She is wrong-headed, not wrong-hearted. The solution to her problem is education. She has to get rid of all that bad knowledge and fill her head with good knowledge. Then all will be well, and she will be a paragon of virtue.

The Socratic theory is quite interesting, and quite wrong. It gives a distorting emphasis to the role of knowledge in ethics. That knowledge is critically important in ethics cannot be gainsaid. It is patently evident that we cannot do good unless we know what the good is. So, speaking technically, we say that knowledge is a necessary condition for virtuous behavior, but it is not a sufficient condition. It is needed, but it is not the only thing that is needed. Without having some idea of justice, I cannot act justly. But I must have more than a knowledge of justice; I must have the will to act on that knowledge, to lift it out of the category of the purely theoretical and carry it into the realm of the practical.

Is there any more familiar, more unsettling, experience that we have to put up with, in retrospect, than the breakdown between knowledge and action? Ah, the discrepancies that can occur between what we know and what we do, or fail to do! Situation Number One: a person is acting, but instead of acting according to what he clearly knows to be the right way to act, he acts in just the opposite way. His actions contradict his knowledge. Such is the case with Ned, as he licks his lips and turns the pages of his older sister's diary, which he knows she regards as super-private, and which, if she knew he was reading, would put him in danger of being subjected by her to severe and perhaps life-threatening bodily damage. And yet, despite his knowledge, he reads on, keeping an ear cocked for the sound of a car pulling into the driveway. Ned does not lack will, but he abuses it, for he employs it to act in a way that contradicts his knowledge. His is the "I shouldn't be doing this but . . ." mode of thinking. We are all personally acquainted with it.

Situation Number Two: a person has clear, unambiguous knowledge of a right thing that is to be done, but he is not doing it. Last Thursday Harold got into an acrimonious argument with his co-worker Bennie. In the heat of the battle, he said some pretty nasty things to Bennie. Harold sits in his office, thinking about this. He knows he owes Bennie an apology. And he knows Bennie is now in his office just down the hall. All he has to do is to walk down the hall and make the necessary apology. But Harold continues to sit in his office, thinking about it. Harold is failing to do the right thing, not for lack of knowledge, but for lack of will.

If the Socratic theory were true, if it were an accurate reflection of actual experience, neither of the situations described above would be possible. Ned would not be leafing through his sister's diary; Harold would not be sitting immobilized in his office.

What do we need to do to prevent the breakdown between knowledge and action? First of all, we need the right kind of knowledge, which is to say, knowledge of what truly constitutes the good. And that knowledge must be clear, unambiguous, and firmly held. But because knowledge in itself is not enough, we need a well-ordered will, a will which can back up and follow through on what we know. Another name for a well-ordered will is virtue. While knowledge of the good, taken alone, offers no guarantee that we will act according to that knowledge, virtue does. Virtue is, in essence, simply the capacity to follow through, to act on what we know.

No progress is possible in the ethical life unless there is full cooperation between intellect and will, between what we know and what we do. Without that cooperation we are in a state of continual war with ourselves, not doing what we should be doing, doing what we shouldn't be doing. We lack psychological and moral integrity. We are bifurcated beings.

But the experience we have been reflecting on here, the discrepancy that can occur between what we know and how we act, does it not contradict the notion that we always act according to what we perceive to be good? No. The manner in which we think about ethical matters is invariably complex; it comes in layers. We are seldom, in a perfectly internally consistent way, "of one mind" when we make our moral choices. Consider the case of Ned again, flipping through the pages of his sister's diary. At one level he knows that what he is doing is wrong— that explains why he is so nervous—but at another, deeper level he perceives it as a good, as something he really wants to do. If he did not, he could not do it. Whenever we say to ourselves, "Yes, I know what I am doing is wrong, but . . . " we can be sure that at a certain level of our consciousness we have effectively rectified the wrong, transforming it in self-serving fashion into a "right," and this twisted transformation then functions as the motivating impetus for our actions. It is what we say to ourselves after the "but" that tells the story.

Thirty-One
Pleasure

Is pleasure a problem for the ethical life? It can be, but it is not necessary that it should be. Ensuring that it is not a problem is simply a matter of taking it for what it is, not making too much of it, nor too little of it. In this instance, as in the ethical life as a whole, the moderate middle course is the one to follow. We must become expert in the rational avoidance of extremes.

One of the extreme attitudes that can be taken toward pleasure, the extreme that makes too much of it, is that of hedonism. The hedonist's translation of "the pursuit of happiness" is "the pursuit of pleasure. He lives for pleasure. Hank, known to his acquaintances as Happy Hank, is a dedicated hedonist. His philosophy of life, such as it is, is summed up in a single monosyllabic word—"fun." Having fun is what it's all about. If you're not having fun, then you're not really living. Hank is not discriminatory in the matter of pleasure; he will take it in just about any form it will present itself. Not that he is particularly grateful for the favors pleasure bestows upon him, convinced as he is that he has them all coming to him. Giving the lie to snide comments to the effect that he is lazy and lacks mental initiative, Hank in fact shows much energy and ingenuity in his relentless pursuit of pleasure. It was only after Hank became a full-time hedonist that he had to discover for himself what the veterans could have told him, that the more pleasure you get, the more you want. This puts you on a treadmill which moves ever faster and faster until it has you running at your top speed, gasping for breath. You can keep that up for only so long. Such was the case with Hank.

I should have used the past tense in what I said above about Hank, for he is no longer with us; the treadmill finally did him in. Hedonism can be hard on the system. Pleasure, taken in extreme doses, has a cruel way of turning into pain. Made the whole purpose of life, it then turns on life and destroys it.

The extreme opposite to hedonism, making too little of pleasure, does not seem to have a commonly agreed-on name. I will call it insensitivity. The insensitive person would be one who takes a totally negative attitude toward pleasure, looking upon it as antithetical to a genuinely ethical life. Pleasure, for him, is the preoccupation of spineless sybarites. To succumb to its sickly charms is to become a weakling. The strong live without pleasure, and they become increasingly stronger because they do so.

The insensitive type can be rather impressive in a fierce, forbidding way, but, as a type, it is rare. The insensitive souls of the world are far outnumbered by the hedonists. It is fairly easy to become a hedonist, but serious insensitivity can be very demanding. No one can live without some pleasure in his life, and to try to do so is to make open war on one's very nature. But that's something hedonism and insensitivity have in common— they both war against the healthily human, though in quite different ways.

Before we address the question of the proper role of pleasure in the ethical life, it is important that we have a precise idea of what we are dealing with. Though the way we commonly talk about it can suggest otherwise, pleasure is not a "thing," a free-standing entity, a substance. Like happiness, pleasure is not "out there" but "in here"; specifically, it is simply a positive psychosomatic response to an action, taken in the broadest sense, as referring to any experience in which we are fully engaged. As such, pleasure always accompanies action, as its effect. The activity of eating is productive of gustatory pleasure, and to some energetic souls jogging is a pleasurable experience. The activity which is productive of pleasure need not be physical activity. We can derive pleasure from solving a purely mental conundrum. Listening to beautiful music can be immensely pleasurable, and as Aristotle observed, one of our greatest pleasures comes from exercising our visual powers; it is a pleasure just to look at things.

Given the fact that pleasure is inseparable from action, when it comes to assessing pleasure from an ethical point of view, applying to it appropriate moral valuation, we need to refer to the action it accompanies, the effect of which it is. In other words, if we want to determine whether a particular pleasure is morally good or bad, we must refer to the particular act that causes it. The formula to be followed here is quite simple: if the act that causes the pleasure is good, the pleasure is good; if the act that causes the pleasure is bad, the pleasure is bad. The altruist can experience pleasure in benefitting others, for which fact he need not blush nor feel compelled to make apologies. The sadist takes pleasure in giving pain to others; his actions are evil, hence the pleasure he derives from them are evil.

The hedonist is dedicated to engaging in pleasure-producing activity only, while eschewing activity that could be productive of pain, whereas the insensitive soul, with equal dedication, attempts to avoid all activity which gives the slightest hint that any pleasure might come along with it.

The right attitude to take toward pleasure should be clear enough. We obviously would not want to have anything to do with the pleasure that accompanies evil acts. As to the pleasure that can accompany good acts, we should be grateful for it. But do we have to remind ourselves that pleasure does not necessarily accompany good acts? That it does not should tell us that our focus must always be on the act itself, not on whatever emotional addenda may come along with it. If we were to choose to do only those good things that we expect will be pleasurable, the amount of good we do would be appreciably reduced. Sometimes doing the right thing can prove to be a rather flat experience, looked at from a purely emotional point of view. Sometimes it can be positively painful.

Thirty-Two

Emotionalism

The ethical life and the rational life are really one and the same. To be a morally upright person is to be a rational person, an eminently sane person. We are by nature rational creatures, but that is not the whole of the story. We are also by nature emotional creatures, and these two aspects of our nature, our rational selves and our emotional selves, do not always get along well with one another. They should, but the disconcerting fact of the matter is that they often do not.

The ideal situation would be this: reason runs the show, is the director of the drama, and the emotions, like conscientious professional actors, follow the script that is provided to them by reason. That reason should rule and the emotions be ruled is one of the central tenets of all the great ethical systems of the world, East and West. Since the very dawn of ethical thought, and with sterling consistency down through the ages, the preponderance of humankind has taken it as axiomatic that the emotions must be governed and guided by reason, otherwise moral problems inevitably ensue.

The emotions must be *governed*, and benevolently, not suffocated or suppressed; they must be *guided*, not disallowed their natural and proper expression. We need to adopt toward the emotions the same balanced, non-extremist attitude we spoke about in discussing pleasure, which is arguably the most potent of our emotions. The emotions are not bad; they only act badly when they are allowed to act on their own, as governing, not governed, when they so assert themselves that they attempt to reorient the direction of a person's entire life. What is especially problematic about such a state of affairs is that the manner of governance exercised by the emotions is ruthlessly anti-democratic; once they gain the upper hand, their management of reason is positively tyrannical.

The ancient Stoic philosophers taught that what we should chiefly strive for in life is inner peace, tranquility of spirit, a state in which we remain calm and self-possessed in the face of whatever slings and arrows outrageous fortune might choose to subject us to. The most important thing for the Stoics was to follow nature, which meant resignedly taking things as they come, faithfully meeting the duties of your life's vocation, and always keeping uppermost in mind the distinction between what is under your control and what is not, giving all your attention to the first, and completely ignoring the second. There is much to admire in the Stoic ideal, but the attitude they took toward the emotions was excessively negative. They advocated a kind of mastery over the emotions which would effectively thwart their natural expression.

Control of the emotions is one thing, and a necessary thing, but it would be going altogether too far to suppose that we should try to quash the emotions, or, more radically, root them out of our system. Even if such a program were to be considered advisable which it definitely is not—it would be impossible to accomplish, and positively dangerous even to attempt. Man has been defined as a rational animal. The "animal" part of the definition implies the emotional dimension of our nature. Willy nilly, we respond feelingly to the world around us, which is simply to say that we respond to it humanly.

Some schools of thought have found the emotion of desire to be particularly problematic. We know desire to be the emotion that drives us toward the good; if it is a real good toward which we are being driven, then we can have full confidence in our chauffeur. But try to imagine what would happen if we were to decide that desire itself is a cause of so much trouble in our lives that we should take measures effectively to root it out of our system. This position is not as outlandish as it may sound, and millions of people, under the sway of Buddhist philosophy, have found something to recommend in it. Desire, they would argue, because of its insatiable character, because it is always fated to be frustrated, is a constant source of unrest for the soul, and therefore should be extirpated. The goal is to reach a state where we are entirely without desire, for in the absence of desire we will find complete inner serenity.

There is something in this point of view that in a moment of weakness I might find persuasive. The emotion of desire, I freely admit, can at times cause me considerable trouble, constantly nagging me with its "I want this!" and "I want that!" And no sooner do I satisfy one desire than two more

come along to take its place. If only I could once and for all extinguish desire, I muse to myself, perhaps I would then know genuine and lasting inner
peace. Perhaps. But at a very great price, for I would have purchased peace
by doing severe, and perhaps irreparable, damage to my human nature. Desire can sometimes lead us astray, putting us in pursuit of things that contradict our genuine best interests, but it is also desire, a well regulated desire,
that puts us in pursuit of the good. Not to desire the good, and want it, is
to be lacking just that kind of aspiration which differentiates us from the
brutes.

Within the past two hundred years or so a novel way of looking at
human emotion has gained a certain amount of currency in ethical thought.
It represents a position which runs directly contrary to the ideas I have been
propounding in this book. In its boldest and uncompromising expression,
it simply rejects the classical notion that reason should be the governing
factor in our lives, and argues for just the opposite: our affective selves
should be given prominence of place in morals. It is the emotions, not reason, that should govern. Put in anatomical terms, heart must take precedence over head; it is not the brain but the gut that should be the seat of
human motivation. We have in our feelings, the argument goes, a totally
reliable, indeed a virtually indefectible, guide for our behavior. If we cared
to research the matter, we could doubtless find the seeds of this frankly un-
natural way of looking at moral agency in ancient times, but in the developed way it now presents itself to us, it is very much a product of the
modern mind. I would generally characterize it as an example of philosophical Romanticism.

The advocates of this point of view urgently recommend that we eman-
cipate ourselves from the constraints placed upon us by the classical position, the adherence to which has schooled us in a way of thinking that
depreciates the importance and proper role of human emotions. We need,
they insist, to restore a correct understanding of reason and emotion. Reason is cold, hard, and insufficiently resilient and adaptable; when it rules it
stifles spontaneity and creative self-expression. Our emotions, on the other
hand, are warm, flexible, and immediately responsive to our deepest personal needs. Our emotions express our truest selves, and following their
lead will allow us to become the person we should want to be.

There is no need to mount complicated arguments to respond to this point of view. If one is the least bit tempted to subscribe to it, all one need do is appeal to common sense and the evidence of one's ordinary experience. Imagine putting it to an empirical test, giving it a sustained try and see what would happen. Imagine the shape your life would quickly take if in fact you decided to allow all of your actions to be dictated by your emotions. Consider the specific emotions of anger, fear, and desire. Ungoverned anger peaks in rage, which unchecked leads to the shutdown of reason and a complete loss of control. We know what the consequences of that could be. Ungoverned fear cripples; the person in the grips of a dominating fear cannot act at all. Ungoverned desire becomes lust, lust for power, lust for sex, lust for lust itself, as desire, consumed by its own fierce fires, runs wild, producing in the end nothing but a pathetic little pile of colorless ash, eventually to be blown away by the desert winds.

Thirty-Three
Fear

Our freedom, which is essential to our identity as moral agents, can, as we saw, be curbed by external factors. The freedom to roam the streets of Rome or Roanoke is severely infringed if I find myself confined to a jail cell. But there are also internal constraints to freedom, one of the most powerful of which is the emotion of fear.

Fear is one of our basic emotions, and, just as such, a good thing. We could not live without it. If you were to try to imagine a completely fearless man, you would have to imagine fast, because he would not be around for very long. Fear is a built-in alarm system, alerting us to potential dangers, so that we can take the kind of action that is appropriate to the real conditions of the situation in which we find ourselves. That is how it works when fear is behaving as it should behave, under the control of reason. Rational fear is always on our side. Irrational fear is one of the biggest problems we have to deal with in attempting to live ethically.

The most common source of fear is self-doubt. We begin to question our ability to achieve a difficult good, or to escape from a particularly potent evil. Fear of this kind is quite common, for we often find ourselves in situations where a goal we have set for ourselves, after we have unsuccessfully given considerable effort to achieving it, begins to look as if it is beyond our reach. Or we begin to wonder, ensconced in a particularly bad situation, if we might be hopelessly stuck in it. In either case the fear could be called rational in the sense that it is alerting us to real, not just imagined, difficulties. But if not kept on a tight leash by reason, fear can severely distort any situation to which it is responding. Overly influenced by fear, I can underestimate my own capacities either to achieve a difficult goal or to extricate myself from a sorry state of affairs. One way or the other, fear can force us to give up too soon.

Jerome is desperately in love with the lovely Jennifer. His long-range plan regarding her terminates in matrimony, but he knows that he has a long row to hoe before that celestial consummation arrives, should it ever arrive. Jerome thinks, earnestly hopes, that Jennifer, at least at some undoubtedly lower level of intensity, reciprocates his affection. But he has his doubts, about that and a lot of other things. The comparisons he often makes between himself and her are not great confidence builders. He is reasonably intelligent, but she is Phi Beta Kappa, *summa cum laude*, and has a full scholarship to grad school; he is a respectable conversationalist, but she is positively scintillant; he is a good athlete, but she can wipe up the court with him in tennis; he could pass for being respectably good-looking, but she is radiantly beautiful. And so on. Has it ever so much as crossed her mind, Jerome wonders, to think of him as a possible husband? And he worries about that shy, sly way she sometimes has of looking at his best friend, Craig. Will Jerome ever win the hand of Jennifer? Because he has his doubts, he has his fears.

We can fear that we might not be able to hold on to what we already have. Bertrand is the undisputed heavyweight champion of the world. He has won the crown for seven spectacular years straight, defending it twice in each of those years—14 bouts, 12 of them won by knockouts. Bertrand made a solemn promise to his mother, as she lay on her deathbed, that he would be champion of the world for 10 years, and that he would then retire with a perfect record, undefeated, never having had his knees buckled by an opponent. But recently Bertrand has begun to worry. In his most recent bout it took 11 rounds before he could put the challenger away. And then there is that young Moriarity, constantly pestering him for a bout. The kid looks tough, a bit too tough. Bertrand is having doubts that he will be able to hang on to the crown for the ten years he promised his mother it would be his. More and more he finds himself mentally shadowboxing with fear, which deftly feints, bobs, and weaves and threatens to put him on the canvas.

A certain amount of controlled fear works to our benefit, keeping us on the *qui vive*. But uncontrolled fear, which is to say, fear that is *in* control, incapacitates us. We are helpless so long as we are in the grips of it, and that would render an ethical life very difficult, if not impossible, for only free people can live ethical lives, and the freedom of a person debilitated by fear is in question. The remedy for uncontrolled fear is the virtue of fortitude.

The *virtue* of fortitude. A virtue is a peculiar kind of strength, a firmly established enabling capacity that bucks up the will and provides us with what we need in order to follow through on our knowledge of the good. The ethical life is a balanced life, we know, a life characterized by behavior that avoids extremes of excess or defect. In the case of fortitude, or courage, it is a mean between the defective extreme of timidity, on the one hand, and the excessive extreme of recklessness on the other. The timid person pays too much attention to fear, and does not do the right thing when the right thing is clearly his to do. The reckless person, for his part, does not pay enough attention to fear and, heedless of its reasonable warnings, rushes into situations thoughtlessly. If he manages to survive the experience, the situation he was responding to is very often made worse as the result of his precipitant intervention. True courage avoids the extremes of timidity and recklessness.

Fortitude does not eradicate fear, it tames it, makes it manageable, enables us to act, and act decisively, not because we have no fear, but in spite of the fear we have. We tend to associate courage with headline heroics, but the courage most people are called upon to display most of the time goes unreported and often unnoticed: facing difficult situations without being intimidated by them, doing the right thing simply because it is the right thing to do. The most heroic brand of courage is displayed by those who, with quiet, uncomplaining patience, bear evils, physical or otherwise, from which they cannot escape and over which they have no control. Though perhaps broken in body, they remain unbroken in spirit. These people are moral giants.

As for Bertrand the boxer, he could take a page from the book of the Stoics, and work on developing that calm fortitude which allows us to accept the bad with the good. He should give it everything he's got to honor that solemn promise he made to his mother, but if giving it everything he's got proves not to be enough to allow him to fulfill that promise, then Bertrand is just going to have to take it on the chin, and learn how to be defeated without being defeated. And Jerome? His worst fears were realized: those shy, sly glances Jennifer was casting toward his friend Craig were meaningful in ways that eventually led to their marriage. But to love and lose, and not have the loss become the occasion for wallowing in self-pity, is a result which courage would have an important hand in effecting.

The cases of Jerome and Bertrand, you might be thinking, do not represent the most earthshaking of ethical situations. True enough, at least not from our perspective. But the disinterested onlooker seldom has an adequate idea of the nature and degree of courage that might be called for on the part of people in the peculiar situations in which they find themselves. Courage must be gauged with the psychology of individual differences in mind. A situation which might be no big deal for Jason, making the question of courage almost irrelevant for him, may be a very big deal indeed for Vernon, requiring all the courage he can muster to face up to the situation without quailing.

Worry is a minor form of fear, which is most efficiently handled by not giving it the time of day. Of all the kinds of mental activity we can engage in, worry ranks among the most completely useless. It surely is among the most enervating. Worry tends to assign infallible status to Murphy's Law, and regards future uncertainties as fixed certainties, which are always dire. One recalls Grandma Rush's homey ditty: "Worry is like rocking in a rocking chair, you're doing a lot of moving but not getting anywhere."

Thirty-Four

Ethics and Habit

Being ethical, being morally good, is very much a matter of having good habits. We dub Dan a good man because he displays a steady consistency in his good behavior. There is a set pattern in the way he behaves. He was good man Dan yesterday, he's that today, and we have every reason to expect that he will be so tomorrow. In fact, we can confidently count on it. And the same thing can be said of Sally, a good woman if ever there was one. She is steady and stable in her goodness. We do not consider her to be a good person on account of how she occasionally acts, but on account of how she habitually acts. There is, for us, an edifying regularity in how she goes about living her life.

Good people are clearly and distinctly marked by consistency in the way they act. Where does that consistency come from? It comes from habit. We have seen that, in ethics, knowledge of the good is not enough to ensure good behavior. We need not only to know, we need to be able to act on what we know—promptly, competently, and with ease. It is habit that allows us to do that, for it is habit that props up the will and moves it to act in accord with knowledge. Intellect and will become partners, working hand in hand.

The habits around which the ethical life is built are of course moral habits, habits that govern those acts that are assessable in terms of their being morally good or bad. A good moral habit is one that enables us to act well morally. It ensures good performance in the ethical sphere, in much the same way that a physical habit ensures good performance of a physical activity of one kind or another. In terms of their basic structure, and how they are both formed and deformed, moral habits and physical habits have very much in common.

Just as the musician is artistically good by reason of habit, so too we are morally good by reason of habit. To be habituated to a particular kind of physical activity, like playing the piano, is to have that activity deeply ingrained in us. For Victoria, playing the piano is more than simply something she does; it reveals what she is, what she has become as the result of her own assiduous efforts. She is an artist. Peter plays the piano too, and he is a nice fellow, but we would not call him a pianist, not at any rate in any serious sense, and we would very definitely not call him an artist. He lacks the habit. Comparable to the artistry of music, there is an artistry of morals (it is called virtue), and habit is the explanation for both.

The critically important role ethics attaches to habit underscores its character as a practical science. While we necessarily begin with knowledge of the good, we must move beyond the mere knowledge and learn to act upon it, act upon it in such a way that it eventually becomes so much a part of us that it identifies what we are. Just as Victoria had to habituate herself to the musical good, we must strive to habituate ourselves to the moral good. Like her music, it must become second nature to us.

We are all thoroughly habituated to language, principally in the form of our mother tongue. Most of us became habituated to speaking English at so early an age we cannot recall the process by which it all came about. And now, most of the time we are not even conscious of the fact that we are speaking English. We just do it. It is an activity we engage in continuously and effortlessly. Such is the great benefit of habit.

Those of you who have taken a serious stab at learning a second language as an adult know the work that has to go into forming a new language habit. Despite all the books and programs with titles like *Russian Made Easy, Danish for Dummies*, and *Icelandic for Idiots* which might suggest otherwise, one discovers that there are no shortcuts to learning a second language. It requires much time and concentrated effort. That's the way it is with all habit formation. You know you are making progress with a new language when suddenly whole patches of what were once meaningless sounds now sing with sense, and when you start saying things with a kind of fluency which surprises even yourself. Deep implantation of the habit is beginning to take place.

Despite the similarities in the formation of physical habits and moral habits, there is no automatic carryover effect from the physical to the moral. We are dealing here with two quite different realms, and sometimes, in the very same person, there can be large discrepancies as far as habit formation is concerned. I alluded earlier to a situation where there can be a great artist, an accomplished actor, say, who despite his thespian prowess leaves much to be desired as a human being. He can get standing ovations for his performances on stage, but those who know his daily performances as a person are not inclined to clap.

Thirty-Five
Getting into the Habit

Habits are simply and elegantly divided into the good and the bad. Be they one or the other, they are both formed in precisely the same way. In ethics, we are of course mainly concerned with moral habits; the good ones we call virtues, the bad ones, vices. We are concerned with both.

The process of habit formation is straightforwardly simple; it can be summed up in two words: conscientious repetition. Tommy the Little Leaguer plays center field for the Bay Street Bulldogs. He is a good hitter, fleet of foot, and rarely fails to catch a fly ball, but ground balls are his Achilles' heel. Tommy's coach recognizes the problem and one day he sits down with him and gives him a little lecture on the art of handling ground balls for outfielders. "Keep your eye on the ball; think first about getting hold of it, not what you're going to do with it after you've gotten hold of it; get *behind* the ball, don't come at it from the side; get down on one knee so that if you miss it with your glove your body will block it." And then for several days running he takes Tommy aside and hits ground balls to him, one after another. As these individualized practice sessions continue, Tommy steadily improves; he is fumbling fewer and fewer ground balls, and none are getting by him. Finally, after two weeks of this, Tommy, though no Willie Mays yet, has become pretty proficient at handling ground balls. The foundations of a good habit have been laid. And what did it take on Tommy's part? Conscientious repetition of a certain kind of act.

Learning how to handle ground balls may not be all that important, measured against the great scheme of things, but in terms of the basic principles involved, there is no difference between forming that habit or any other habit, physical or moral. First, you have to have some knowledge of the right actions to be performed, then comes the more important part— the conscientious repetition of those actions until they become so ingrained in you that you can perform them almost automatically. Repetition is the heart of habit formation, but if it is to be effective it cannot be mechanical; the actions must be repeated in an alert, focused fashion. You have to pay close attention to what you are doing, remembering the right way of doing it, not allowing yourself to get lackadaisical or sloppy in your movements, and immediately correcting any mistakes you make. The volitional aspect is very important. You must really want to form the habit. No vacillation, tentativeness, or half-hearted commitment will do here. Only those prepared to be totally dedicated to the task will succeed. It is the firm commitment in the beginning that gives you the perseverance you need to stick with it to the end.

Moral habits are those that make us better, not as center fielders or as pianists or as bakers, but as human beings. They enable us to live in such a way that our actions bring out the best in our nature. The good person is the end toward which all moral habits are directed. Could we be more precise about what we mean by a good person? Consider a particular trait, like generosity, which would be universally recognized as something positive. A good person would be one who, among other positive traits, is generous, a person for whom giving counts more than getting.

But I hear a rather strident objection coming from the back of the hall. "What about people," the objector asks, "who are, as we say, generous to a fault? We wouldn't call them good persons, would we?" "Very probably not," I say to the objector, "and we would be right in hesitating to do so. What kind of person would we identify as being generous to a fault? Would it not be someone who is recklessly extravagant, intemperate in the way he dispenses of his goods? He is thoughtless and promiscuous in his giving. He lacks sound judgment. Now, such a person would not be truly generous because generosity, like every other virtue, always bears upon it the deep impress of rationality, and manifests itself in balanced behavior."

There is common agreement that generosity is a positive human trait, the kind of trait we would expect to find in a good person. And it would be hard to find anyone disagreeing with the proposition that to be habitually generous would be a definite moral asset. Enter Gus. Among other problems, he is a fellow who is decidedly lacking in generosity. He could very much use the habit. How would he go about acquiring it? From a purely operational point of view, he must do as Tommy the dedicated Little Leaguer did: establish a routine of conscientious repetitive behavior. Gus must concentrate on performing generous acts, rather than on those having to do with handling ground balls. He must make a point of not passing up any opportunity for acting generously. More, he must go out of his way to create opportunities for acting generously. In the early stages of the process, things will probably not be easy for Gus. After all, he lacks the habit of generosity. However, if he keeps at it, acting generously will become increasingly less difficult for him. A different Gus will begin to emerge, a magnanimous chap the likes of which we never knew before.

In forming good moral habits, we never start completely from scratch. We always have a certain amount of raw material, in the form of natural dispositions, the givens of our temperamental makeup which, depending on whether they are positive or negative, we work either with or against. I will consider two cases to illustrate the point, those of Baird and Barbara, both having to do, once again, with forming the habit of generosity. Baird, as it happens, was stingy by nature. He knew that, was not pleased by it, and was determined to do something about it. Because of his temperamental propensity toward stinginess, he had to put extra effort into becoming a generous person, for he not only had to implant some favorable flora (generosity), he also had to uproot some rank weeds (stinginess). But he went about it with gusto, and eventually succeeded in forming the virtue of generosity.

Then there is Barbara, who is one of those naturally generous types. She seems to have been born that way. When she was a little girl she drove her parents to distraction by her free-wheeling magnanimity. "Barbara, where is your Barbie doll?" "I gave it to Dora." "Barbara, where is your tricycle?" "I gave it to Stevie." Because of her natural disposition for generosity, acquiring the habit was a relatively easy matter for her.

But why, you might wonder, if Barbara had a natural disposition for generosity, did she have to bother about acquiring the habit in the first place? Because a natural disposition, good or bad, is not the same thing as a habit, good or bad. The key difference between the two is that a natural disposition is simply a given, part of our genetic package, as it were. A habit, on the other hand, is something that we acquire through conscious effort. The reason why even someone like Barbara, with her natural disposition for generosity, has to acquire the habit of generosity, is because habits are decidedly more dependable than dispositions. A positive temperamental proclivity may or may not display itself in a situation where it needs to be displayed; it all depends on the present mood of the person with that proclivity. When we describe people as being "temperamental" we refer to the fact that their behavior is erratic and unpredictable. When Barbara had only the natural temperamental proclivity to rely on, she was generous when she felt like it, and wasn't when she didn't. But once she acquired the habit of generosity, that instability in her behavior disappeared. She became consistently and predictably generous. And then there is this consideration: if Barbara never acquired the virtue of generosity, she might very well have ended up as one of those "generous to a fault types" we discussed above.

Natural dispositions, temperamental traits, taken just in themselves, are neither morally good nor bad. It is how we handle them that introduces moral considerations. Our moral status depends on free choices, and we do not freely choose the temperaments we are born with. Baird was not a bad person because he was naturally inclined toward stinginess, nor, for that matter, was Barbara a good person, in an unqualified sense, because of her natural disposition toward generosity. Baird would have become a person of questionable moral standing had he consciously given in to his weakness to the point where, over time, he became habituated to it. Barbara became an unqualifiedly good person once she locked her positive natural disposition firmly in place by habituating herself to it.

For all of us, the temperamental traits with which we are born are a mixed bag, containing both the positive and the negative. Again, think of them in terms of raw material. The idea, of course, is to habituate ourselves to the positive traits and root out the negative ones, or at least keep them under the most rigid control possible. Baird was saddled with that negative inclination toward stinginess, but he was blessed with a large amount of natural courage, so the formation of the habit of courage was not a great struggle for him. Barbara, on the other hand, for whom the forming the habit of generosity was a breeze, had her hands full in learning courage, for by disposition she was a timid person, easily given to fear.

A brief word on the preservation of habits. A good habit, once it is put in place, will not stay in place unless it is kept in place. And it is kept in place by continuing to perform, conscientiously, the kinds of acts that initially established the habit. When it comes to good habits, we can never rest on our laurels, never allow ourselves to think that once the job is done we no longer have to give it any attention. Victoria, polished pianist that she is, will not remain such unless she continuously practices. Practice, we are told, makes perfect. I know an accomplished musician who offers what he considers to be a more apt substitute for that venerable adage: *Perfect* practice makes perfect. That would nicely apply to the moral habits; if we want to keep them, we must keep at them. Neither Baird nor Barbara will maintain a firm hold on the habit of generosity if they do not continue to act generously.

Thirty-Six

Getting Out of the Habit

Needless to say, it is only bad habits that we would want to get out of. A bad moral habit is a fixed disposition that prevents us from being what we ought to be as human beings. Bad habits are consciously and willingly formed; if that were not the case, they would not be habits. They are formed by the repetition of bad acts. Edwina became a habitual liar by telling a lot of lies, knowingly and deliberately. We cannot become genuinely morally good, nor morally bad, by accident. Our moral status is not something that just happens to us. We very much have a say in the matter.

Though both good and bad moral habits are formed in essentially the same way—by the conscientious repetition of a certain type of act—yet there is a difference between the two in that bad habits are more often stumbled into rather than leapt into, are, in other words, more the result of carelessness than thoughtfulness. The analogy with physical habits helps to see how this is so. Most bad physical habits seem to sneak up on us, and it is often only after they have us in their grip that we become fully aware of the fact. A professional golfer can pick up a bad physical habit that will adversely affect his game, but it is hard to imagine that it was something he consciously set about to acquire.

A bad moral habit, for its part, is something for which we are morally responsible. Whatever the degree and intensity of the consciousness that went into its formation, there had to be sufficient awareness, on the part of the person, of the nature and import of the actions he was performing, to justify the judgment that he was morally responsible for those actions. Again, we can only be accounted morally bad if we are responsible for the bad actions that made us so.

We need only to remind ourselves of what causes bad habits to have the key to getting rid of them. Because bad habits are put in place by the repetition of bad acts, the first and obvious order of business, if we want to get rid of those habits, is to stop performing the acts which are responsible for them. On the positive side, we then embark upon a program whereby we perform good acts that are contrary to the kind of bad acts we used habitually to perform.

I made passing reference above to Edwina, an inveterate liar. One day she was sitting in a beauty salon, idly flipping through a magazine, waiting to have her hair done. Suddenly she sat up straight in the chair, closed the magazine, and said, out loud, "That's it! No more! I'm going to change my life!" Everyone looked at her. What had happened at that critical moment was that Edwina had just experienced an epiphany. She decided, point blank, then and there, that she had had quite enough with the tawdry business of lying. She was going to stop being a liar and become a truthful person. And she did it. The task was by no means an easy one for her, but the process she had to follow was simple enough. First of all, she stopped telling lies, cold turkey. That was an especially hard part for, remember, she was a habitual liar, meaning that she was rather good at it. There were occasions when she had some real stretchers at the tip of the tongue, and had to bite her tongue to keep them back. And there were times when one or two minor fibs would slip out before she could stop them, but she eventually controlled that. As for the positive side of the program, Edwina made a concerted effort to be rigorously truthful in all of her dealings with others. It took a while, but the effort she put into ridding herself of a bad moral habit and replacing it with a good one eventually proved fruitful. Edwina ended up an honest woman, thoroughly dependable and trustworthy. She was so honest she would even tell people her age, without being asked.

At whatever point in our lives we might find ourselves when it dawns on us that the ethical life needs to be taken seriously, even if we are quite young at the time, we already have a history behind us, relatively short though it might be. In embarking upon the great humanizing adventure of pursuing the good we have to take that history into account. We start forming habits, good and bad, very early in the game of life, and those habits, perhaps because we are so impressionable at that stage, seem to be more tenacious than those formed in later years. This is good news if the habits are good, not so good if they are bad.

There is a danger in taking too pessimistic an attitude toward bad moral habits which are formed in our early years, estimating them to be virtually ineradicable, and thus looking upon ourselves as in effect morally hobbled for life. It would be unrealistic to discount the difficulties involved in uprooting bad habits formed in early life, but it would be fatalistic to take them to be beyond remedy. It is common knowledge that good moral habits which are formed in early life can be lost. Nothing logically prohibits, then, the shedding of bad habits which are formed in early life. Considerations of this sort naturally point to the importance of an education that does not limit itself to the development of the mind, but looks to the whole person, and seeks to present to the world young people who have developed good moral habits as well as good intellectual habits, who are both smart and virtuous.

Thirty-Seven
Virtue

Virtue is the name ethics gives to good moral habits; bad moral habits are collectively called vices. Because both are habits, virtue and vice together bear the mark of permanency, which is either a blessing or a curse, depending on what kind of moral habit is at issue. Virtue and vice are stable states of moral being, not fleeting phases in a person's life. Accordingly, we speak of virtuous or vicious people, those who are identified, gladly or sadly as the case might be, by the kind of behavior to which they have habituated themselves.

Our English word "virtue" has its roots in the Latin *virtus*, one of the basic meanings of which is "strength." Virtue, then, is a peculiar kind of strength, an enabling capacity which permits a person to act consistently, and with facility, in ways that are consonant with human reason. Because virtue is a habit, an ingrained disposition, it is ever ready-to-hand for the virtuous person, to be called upon as need arises. Virtue ensures action, the right kind of action—therein lies its paramount feature. We know virtuous people by their actions, and we can benefit significantly from that knowledge. We can learn more about virtue by observing how virtuous people behave than by reading all the ethics books in the world, including this one.

Again, permanency of possession is one of the key features of virtue, but this does not mean that virtuous people never stumble in leading an upright life. When they do, however, they act out of character, and we do not conclude that they have ceased to be virtuous. When a star quarterback throws a couple of interceptions in a game, we do not peremptorily demote him from star status, despite the fact that one of those interceptions was run back for a touchdown. Even the pros have bad days. Similarly, a virtuous person can slip and fall on occasion, by performing a non-virtuous act. But that non-virtuous act does not undo him as a virtuous person. A good habit is not destroyed by a single bad act, any more than it was put in place by a single good act. And precisely because a virtuous person is one who is *habituated* to virtue, it is the habit that is going to get him right back on his feet again after the fall. The same principle applies to the quarterback who had a bad day on the field with his two interceptions. The next week he throws five touchdown passes, runs for over a hundred yards, and leads his team to a glorious victory over a shell-shocked opponent. Habit guarantees comeback.

There is a whole array of specific moral virtues, the good habits that determine good behavior, but there are four of them in particular which enjoy very special status in ethics. They are called the cardinal virtues, and they are: prudence, justice, fortitude, and temperance. The prominence of place given to them is explained by the fact that these are the most basic of the moral virtues, in that they cover every major aspect of the ethical life. They are also regarded as the most basic because all the other moral virtues derive from them, as being special expressions of one or another of the cardinal virtues. So, for example, understanding is a special expression of prudence, and perseverance is a special expression of fortitude. The cardinal virtues have played a prominent role in ethical thought for centuries, and Cicero, the statesman, philosopher, and famed orator of ancient Rome, has left us some valuable commentaries on them.

Each of these cardinal virtues—"cardinal" because they are the virtues on which all the others hinge (*cardo* is the Latin word for hinge)—merits a short description. Prudence is the chief of the cardinal virtues; is, in fact, the chief of all of the moral virtues, in that it governs them all. Prudence enables us to think clearly and decisively about all matters pertaining to morality. The prudent person carefully settles upon, case by case, the right thing to do, the wrong thing to avoid doing. Prudence is reason at work within the moral realm. To act ethically is to act in accordance with reason, and prudence is the virtue that makes that possible.

There is a tendency in the popular mind to reduce prudence to something like carefully calculated caution, thus to advise someone to "be prudent" might be understood to mean, "watch your step, measure your words carefully, don't do anything that could jeopardize your position. While caution can be considered to be a part of prudence, it is by no means the whole of it. Prudence is comprehensive in scope, and to be prudent means to be ethically intelligent across the board.

Justice is the social virtue by which we are enabled to deal fairly and squarely with one another on a day-to-day basis. It is a virtue which is absolutely incompatible with a self-serving individualism. Justice is traditionally defined as "giving everyone his due," that is, paying out to every person what we owe to them, in whatever particular manner that needs to be done. The most basic obligation of justice is to render to every person the respect due them simply by reason of their status as persons. Determining what is due to others in specific terms and in varying situations can at times be quite challenging, and prudence must often give assistance to justice in making those determinations. The just person has a keen sense of the obligations he has toward others with regard to the various ways they relate to him, as his peers, as those who are dependent upon him (e.g., as children or employees), and as those who hold positions of legitimate authority over him and to whom he therefore owes respect and appropriate allegiance.Earlier we observed that fortitude is the virtue which enables us to do what needs to be done for the sake of the good in those situations where we have to contend with the possible impeding influence of the emotion of fear. The essence of fear, as we saw, is the second-guessing of our capacity to act effectively when confronting a good which is difficult to attain, or an evil which is difficult to avoid. Fear which is kept under reasonable control can be a stimulant to effective action, but if it breaks free of the control of reason and becomes the dominant factor in our lives, effective action is diminished, if not rendered altogether impossible. It is the virtue of fortitude that enables us to act rightly in spite of whatever fear might be badgering us, attempting to divert us from our purposes. While not removing fear, fortitude domesticates it, preventing it from going wild. Fortitude takes many forms, one of the most impressive of which, as noted previously, is the patience which enables us to endure evils we cannot escape, but by which we are not broken.

It is the mark of every virtue that it provides us with the capacity to avoid the extremes of action, striking the balance between defective acts, where we don't do enough, and excessive acts, where we overdo it, in either case not meeting circumstances as they need to be met. The specific task of temperance, the fourth of the cardinal virtues, is to give us the wherewithal to lead a balanced life with regard to pleasure. The temperate person is one who avoids the extreme of making pleasure the sole reason for acting or refraining from acting, while at the same time avoiding the opposite extreme of looking upon pleasure as a veritable evil, and therefore as antithetical to the ethical life as such. Because temperance knows pleasure to be inseparably linked with action, as its effect, it keeps focused on action, and determines the goodness or badness of pleasure by the goodness or badness of the action that causes it.

The moral virtues stand or fall together; you cannot be in real possession of any one of them without being in possession of the rest of them as well. The human person, as a moral agent, is all of a piece, an integral whole. Given how virtue relates to person, it is inconceivable, from a psychological point of view, that someone could be, let us say, truly just, and yet at the same time be totally bereft of fortitude and temperance. And given the special role of prudence, as the queen of the moral virtues, if a person possesses prudence, that person would have the full panoply of virtues. Would that person have all of the virtues in exactly the same degree? No. But no single virtue would be completely absent.

Thirty-Eight
Freedom and Responsibility

Because it is so important, allow me to repeat, with Latinate emphasis, the point that free will is a *conditio sine qua non*—in English, an absolutely essential condition—for ethics. To rephrase the point in plainer, more concise terms: no freedom, no ethics. Like the horse and carriage combination, you can't have one (ethics) without the other (freedom). That is, or at least it should be, an obvious point, but then the obvious, often simply by reason of its very obviousness, has a way of dipping below our visual horizon.

Responsibility goes hand in hand with freedom. What underlies and animates a vibrant sense of responsibility is the certain knowledge that, because we are the originating source of our actions, we are answerable for them. If any act I perform is a voluntary act, in the sense spelled out earlier—i.e., I know exactly what I am doing in performing a given act and I clearly will what I am doing—then I have to bear the responsibility for that act, for better or for worse. If it was a bad act, then I must hang my head in shame and accept the blame for it. However, if perchance the act happened to be a meritorious one, then it would be petulant of me not to accept with grace whatever accolades might be directed my way, just so I don't allow them to turn my head.

Praise or blame. These are the spontaneous, perfectly natural responses which pay due respect to the fact of human responsibility, firmly founded upon the more fundamental fact of human freedom. We would very much like, at least in certain of our less presentable moods, to have the freedom without the responsibility, but it is either both or neither. When I do something right, I seldom have any hesitancy in claiming my status as a responsible moral agent. But when I make a mess of things, I have a way of wanting to wiggle out of my responsibility for having done so. And the very idea of human freedom may suddenly become, quite conveniently, a point worthy of serious philosophical debate.

It is not that I am prepared to deny all causal efficacy to the moral agent, but causality as applied to human action, I argue, is a complicated matter. Granted, I was what might be called the immediate, instrumental cause of the dubious deed now under examination, but my meager act was but the final link in a long, complex network of causes which, if we were being properly scientific, should be the focus of our attention. The upshot of any clear-eyed dispassionate analysis of my action, I continue the argument, is that I am not to be held responsible for it, at least not in any narrow, exclusive way. But you still insist on fixing blame? Well, all right, but in doing so push the kind of analysis I am recommending here to its logical terminus. Let's get to the very bottom of things: it's the Big Bang that is ultimately to blame for my errant behavior.

The rule of parsimony, also known as Occam's Razor, which usually makes for good science, may profitably be called into play in relation to this discussion. Of two possible explanations for any given phenomenon, it is the wiser course, all things being equal, to adopt the simpler one. Let us say that thirty-six people saw Fremont doing Act X. In their efforts to come up with a reasonable explanation for that fact, they could: (a) deny that Fremont is a free agent, affirm that he was totally determined by forces entirely beyond his control in performing the act, and then launch into a detailed account of all the putative impersonal causes that made Fremont do what he did, the delineation of which would necessarily involve much heavy conjecture; or (b) modestly suggest that the best explanation for Fremont's doing Act X is that he chose to do it, and that therefore he is responsible for it: a clean slice by Occam's Razor.

Is it really the case that we are not responsible for the acts we perform, and therefore not blameworthy if those acts have negative repercussions? There are theorists who seriously maintain that this is indeed the case. But one cannot help noticing that there is often a discrepancy at work between theory and practice. Professor Pungent will solemnly assure us that we are not responsible for our actions, but try stomping on the professor's toes sometime and see what happens. It is *you* who becomes the immediate focus of his wrath, as he blames you for your act with merciless intensity, while you are vainly trying to explain to him that the devil made you do it.

We are constantly blaming people for the way they behave: the shortstop for throwing to the wrong base and missing a double play; the oboist for sounding a false note, the violinist for coming in a beat too soon; the meteorologist for being way off on his forecast; the preacher for preaching false doctrine or insipid pap; the poet for offering us literary fare which is unpleasing and unmemorable; the plumber for failing to fix the leak; the philosopher for obscurantism; the politician for, well, acting like a politician. Et cetera. On rare occasions, when we are in either an especially magnanimous or penitential mood, we might even voluntarily blame ourselves for things. Think of how pallid and lifeless our language would become, how dull and anemic our conversation, not to say how sparse, if we deleted from it all blaming discourse. The only circumstance that would justify purging all negative judgments from our minds would be our arriving at the transforming conviction that everything and everyone in the world is perfectly and emphatically *okay*, providing no cause for blame, and prompting us to say nothing but nice things about everything and everyone.

Both praise and blame can, obviously, be misapplied. Sinners can be wrongly praised, and saints can be wrongly blamed, but that says nothing about the inherent rightness of praise and blame, rightly applied. An algorithm is not to be rejected because an incompetent works it wrongly. We are justified in employing blaming language because there are certain human actions which are truly blameworthy. And every time we blame a truly blameworthy action we are attesting to the reality of human responsibility and, behind that, human freedom.

But there, in the back row, I see a hand waving frenetically. I invite the energetic waver to speak.

"All I want to say," he says, "is that contrary to what you seem to be intimating here, I simply do not believe that there is such a thing as a bad person."

"Do you believe that there are such things as bad actions?" I ask.

"Bad actions, yes, I'll accept that," he answers.

"But not bad persons?" I ask.

"No," he answers.

"Do you have anything further to say on this matter?" I ask.

"No," he answers.

A brief comment on the above exchange. I would want only to propose the proposition that the peculiar quality of an effect can only be explained by the presence of that same peculiar quality in the cause. If the cause in question is a human agent, then the actions habitually performed by that agent serve to impress an identifying stamp on the agent. For example, we call a cellist someone who habitually plays the cello, a novelist someone who habitually writes novels. Accordingly, it does not seem to be a flagrant violation of logic or language to call someone who habitually performs bad actions—please note that "habitually"—a bad person. In defending that designation I am not claiming that a bad person is bad by nature, but rather by practice. Nor am I claiming that the not-to-be-recommended status of "bad person" is permanent or irrevocable, but only that it is real, and that someone who has that status will retain it for as long as the habitual bad behavior which is responsible for it continues.

When we are fully and healthily conscious of ourselves as responsible moral agents, our actions are inspirited and spurred on by a sharp, abiding sense of "ought." Wherever we go, whatever we do, we bear the burden of obligation. But, happily, obligation is one of those burdens which, in the bearing thereof, we are strengthened rather than enervated. To do what we really ought to do is to act in accordance with what we really are—rational creatures whose freedom is exercised in the service of reason.

Thirty-Nine
Rights

There are very few of us who are not sensitively and protectively conscious of what we identify as our rights. What is a right? We may begin by saying that, like a virtue, it is a personal possession, but whereas all natural virtues come into our possession as the result of studied, steady effort on our part, rights, at least the most important of them, are pure gift. They are ours simply by reason of our being human. Considered generally, a right can be said to be a privilege and a power to act in a certain specified way. The right of free speech, for example, is the privilege and the power to exercise, in the public forum, one's linguistic capacities for the purpose of promulgating and/or defending the truth.

There are two basic kinds of rights, natural and civil. Natural rights, as their name suggests, are ours by nature; we are born with them, and they are thus part of the standard equipment of being human. These are the "pure gift" rights alluded to just above. Because natural rights are part and parcel of what we are as human beings, it is a monumental mistake for anyone to suppose that they can be either conferred upon us or withheld from us by any human individual or human agency.

When Thomas Jefferson, in the *Declaration of Independence*, cites the triad of "life, liberty, and the pursuit of happiness," he is referring to natural rights. When he describes these rights as belonging to people as "endowed by their Creator," he is calling attention to the fact that they do not have their source in any human agency, and when he identifies them as "inalienable" he is making the point that they cannot be taken away from us. It was no accident that Jefferson gave primacy of place to the right to life, for it is the most fundamental of the natural rights. If the right to life is not honored, then of course all the other rights are automatically rendered null and void.

The principal difference between a natural right and a civil right is that the latter, unlike the former, is in fact conferred upon us by a human agency of one sort or another. I was not born with the right to vote in civil elections in the state of Minnesota, even though that is where I began my earthly career. The right to vote was first conferred on me by the appropriate authorities in the northernmost of the contiguous forty-eight states, and only after I had met a number of specified conditions. I was not born with the right to operate a motor vehicle upon the public highways and byways of America. This is a right I had to earn, by passing tests that showed I had an adequate theoretical knowledge of the relevant traffic laws, as well as the practical knowledge which allows me to drive a car with sufficient competence so as not to jeopardize unduly the lives and limbs of my fellow citizens.

Natural rights and civil rights relate to one another in this very important way: natural rights are the source and foundation of civil rights. A natural right, if it is truly that, cannot be anything but genuine. This is not the case, however, with civil rights; they can be specious, even though a society may give them legal status. A so-called civil right is specious, or fictitious, if it has no obvious connection with any natural right.

Having thrown open wide the windows to his apartment, Walter set the powerful speakers of his state-of-the-art sound system on the sills, then put on Beethoven's Ninth Symphony and turned up the volume full blast— all this at 2:00 a.m. This caused not a little consternation among Walter's red-eyed neighbors. When the police arrived on the scene, Walter calmly explained to them, referencing Thomas Jefferson, the logic of his position. "In the actions I took I was but exercising my natural and inalienable right to pursue happiness, and playing Beethoven at full blast over the rooftops of the world at 2:00 a.m. is my idea of happiness." As it happened, the policeman whom Walter was addressing had studied logic in college, and in short order he highlighted a number of fallacies with which Walter's reasoning was burdened. The policeman pointed out that the right to which Walter was laying claim—which the officer aptly described as "the right wantonly to disturb the peace at the behest of whim"—was entirely figmental, and could not therefore be regarded as a legitimate corollary of Walter's natural right to pursue happiness. In exchange for Walter's promise not to repeat the offense, he was let off with a warning and not issued a citation for disturbing the peace.

If I were not free to exercise a right, then that right would be of no practical benefit to me. But my freedom to exercise my rights is not un-conditional. No freedom is unconditional. First of all, and apropos of the point illustrated just above, I have no freedom at all to exercise a specious right, a right, that is, which does not have its source and foundation in a natural right. But neither do I have untrammeled freedom to exercise any genuine right, be it natural or civil. My freedom is limited by the critical condition that in the exercise of any of my rights I not infringe upon the legitimate rights of others. Walter has the right to listen to whatever music he pleases on his state-of-the-art sound system, but not in such a manner that it violates the right of his neighbors to get a good night's sleep. Question: What virtue might it be that would enable us unfailingly to exercise our rights in such a way that in doing so we refrain from treading on the rights of others? Answer: Prudence.

There is the closest kind of connection between rights and responsibility. Each of us is responsible, first, for the proper exercise of our rights and, second, for the recognition and honoring of the rights of others. Rights can be abused. The most obvious way this is done is by exercising them in ways that infringe upon the rights of others. We can also abuse legitimate rights by deliberately going beyond the bounds of what a rational exercise of those rights would entail. For example, I would be abusing my legitimate right to operate a motor vehicle if I were habitually to park on the sidewalk, neg-lect to turn on my headlights at night, and drive at 90 mph on the open road at every available opportunity.

A natural right is ours by nature, and inalienable. Your right to life is absolutely inseparable from you yourself. I cannot take that right away from you. But inalienable rights can be flagrantly dishonored. The possibility of being able actually to exercise even the most fundamental of human rights very much depends on the attitude that others are going to take toward that right. In other words, I have the responsibility, a responsibility of the most solemn kind, (a) simply to recognize the existence of another person's right to life, and then, most importantly, (b) to *honor* that right. What does it mean for me to honor a right? It means that I do nothing which would render impossible, or in any way make difficult, the free exercise of that right.

What holds true for the right to life holds true for every authentic right, natural or civil. A right which is not honored, that is, whose free exercise is prevented, is for all *practical* purposes a non-existent right. It remains true that natural rights are inalienable, but an inalienable right that cannot be exercised is a right in name only. It is a paper privilege, a power rendered impotent. Such is the heavy weight of responsibility we bear toward one another with respect to the recognition and honoring of rights.

We are free to exercise our rights—they would not be much good to us as rights if that were not the case—but we are not always obliged to exercise them, and that fact is an important dimension of the freedom which is associated with rights. We can, for just cause, choose to waive our rights, or in certain situations to act in ways that endanger them. For example, we can, without acting unethically, choose to put in jeopardy the possibility of our continuing to be able exercise the most fundamental of natural rights, the right to life. Firefighters who put their lives at risk in the effort to save the lives of others are not acting suicidally, but displaying the virtue of courage. And deliberately to lay down one's life for another, to forego one's own right to life so that others can continue freely to exercise their right to life—this has traditionally been regarded as one of the most noble acts a human being can perform.

Forty

Conscience

A conscientious person—i.e., a person with a healthy conscience—is for all practical purposes pretty much the same thing as a prudent person. A healthy conscience? Does that imply that it has its opposite in what could be dubbed an unhealthy conscience? It does.

Of all the items pertaining to the ethical life about which there seems to be an inordinate amount of confusion, the idea of conscience ranks very near the top of the list. Among other problems, we have a tendency to imagine conscience as if it were something like a sidekick to our psyche, a kind of companion spirit, providing us with friendly enlightenment and advice to ensure that we stay on the straight and narrow path. We are wont to speak of the "voice" of conscience, or, more poetically, "that still, small voice within," with the intimation that the voice might actually belong to somebody else. It is not that we must swear off trying to be poetical, and stop referring to the "voice" of conscience, only that we be mindful of the fact that the voice we are listening to is our own.

Your conscience is simply *you* or, more precisely, it is you as engaged in a particular kind of mental activity. When you act conscientiously, when you exercise your conscience, what you are doing is performing a specific kind of mental act, making an intellectual judgment, which is an evaluative decision whereby you distinguish between moral right and wrong. That is the essence of what we call conscience. To "follow one's conscience," then, is simply to behave in accordance with the distinctions made by an intellectual judgment, doing what is morally right, avoiding what is morally wrong.

Conscience is not indefectible. How could it be? The essence of conscience is an intellectual judgment. We would certainly be reluctant to say that human intellectual judgments are not subject to error. Therefore, we could not reasonably argue that things should be different in this respect with regard to those cases where the intellectual judgments pertain only to moral matters, that is, when they are specifically judgments of conscience. We are continuously making intellectual judgments regarding a wide variety of matters—history, politics, economics, art, sports, the profession we belong to, the trade we practice, the hobby we follow, and on and on. Dare we claim sweeping indefectibility for those judgments? We like to think that in making them we are right more times than we are wrong, but we know that we can sometimes be way off base even in judgments regarding non-moral matters about which we know a great deal. If that is true about intellectual judgments in general, there is nothing to prevent our being wrong in our judgments pertaining specifically to moral matters, judgments of conscience. We can be wrong about right and wrong.

What is happening, at the most basic level, when I make a bad conscience judgment is that I am simply failing to distinguish correctly between right and wrong. If I were to do this habitually, as a matter of course, I would be burdened with an unhealthy conscience. I would be lacking the virtue of prudence, and that would mean that, in the specific choices I make, I would be mistaking an apparent good for a real good, taking the counterfeit for the genuine.

It is a proverbial dictum of ethics that we must always follow our conscience. We really have no choice in the matter. If we are to act as moral agents at all, we must use our reason in order to make determinations regarding what is morally right and wrong, and then we must abide by those determinations. Not to comply with the intellectual judgments we make regarding moral matters would be like disregarding any other kind of practical judgment we make. Florence, on her way to Sesame Street, sincerely believing that what she is telling herself is true, says: "You have to turn off at Exit 36B if you want to get to Sesame Street," and then, being perfectly conscious of what she is doing, she goes flying right by Exit 36B. That would not make sense, any more than it would make sense to say to yourself, in all sincerity, "Act X is good, do it!" and then not do it, or to say, "Act Y is evil, don't do it!" and then do it.

The obligation always to follow one's conscience rests firmly on the assumption that we are always acting sincerely, that we earnestly believe that the distinction we make, in any given instance between moral right and wrong, is a correct one. But sincerity, though absolutely necessary for a genuinely good act, is not enough, for in itself it does not prevent us from being wrong.

We cannot say with certainty that even the most outrageous historical characters we might name—say Adolf Hitler and Josef Stalin—were not acting sincerely, and that therefore they were not, in that respect, following their consciences. That is exactly what they were doing. And that, rather than preventing them from making some abominable judgments, actually enabled them to do so. What, then, is the explanation for the evil that is done in the name of conscience? Simply this: a corrupt conscience, one that is radically faulty in the moral judgments it makes.

Sincerity and error mix together all too smoothly at times. It is not conscience just as such that guarantees that we do what is right and avoid what is wrong, but only a healthy conscience. It is not sufficient that in our intellectual judgments we distinguish between right and wrong (we invariably do that); those judgments must be correctly made. A healthy conscience is one whose intellectual judgments are sane and rational because they reflect the objective order of things, the way things actually stand in the world which all of us share as moral agents.

Conscience, then, is simply the way we morally evaluate our experiences. Because a *healthy* conscience is practically one and the same with prudence, and because prudence is a virtue, and because a virtue is a habit, and because habits are not something we are born with but which we acquire through our own efforts, it then follows that there is nothing at all automatic about being a conscientious person. It is a status which we must work hard to achieve, and then work hard to maintain. And we can easily see how the whole process must begin very early in the game of life. Hence, once again, the importance of education.

Forty-One

Does Outcome Count as Everything?

One of the ways we regularly exercise our conscience is by reviewing our past actions and evaluating them in terms of their moral quality. "Did I do the right thing in granting that major loan to Jim Jutsen, knowing that there is a likely possibility that he is going to use the money for suspicious purposes?" "Was I too harsh in giving Miss Swanson an 'F' on the midterm math exam? I could have justified a 'D', and maybe with that she would not have quit college and joined a traveling carnival." "How truthful was I in making out my income tax this year?" These are the kinds of questions we ask ourselves when we engage in that soul-searching activity commonly referred to as the examination of conscience. Here we are standing in judgment of ourselves, assessing our own actions from a moral point of view, and then drawing up for ourselves something like a moral report card. The benefit of this exercise is that it allows us to keep close tabs on our judgments of conscience. If I should discover, after reviewing a set of past judgments, that a significant number of them were questionable, or worse, clearly wrong, then I have cause for concern. A healthy conscience, like a healthy body, can only be kept healthy by giving it constant attention.

When we examine our conscience we are dealing with history. The die has been cast, the deed has been done, not to be undone, be it for good or ill. Important though this retrospective way of exercising our conscience is, the more important way has to do with those judgments that are made before, not after, the fact. In this case the good lies vibrantly before us, an inviting promise. Though the future is never completely in our hands, neither is it completely beyond our control.

May I introduce a gentleman with the formidable name of Theodosius who, as convenience would have it, is just at this moment exercising his conscience in the future-oriented way just described. He is contemplating a certain act, which we will unimaginatively call Act X, and he is wondering about its propriety. Act X does not represent a trivial matter, and that is why Theodosius is giving such serious thought to it. He asks himself: Is Act X the right thing to do? And in posing that question he is preparing himself for making a judgment of conscience, by which he will attach a moral value to Act X. If he judges that it is the right thing to do, then he will do it, whereas if Act X receives a negative moral evaluation, then he most certainly will not do it.

What are the kinds of things that Theodosius would have to consider as he tries to determine whether a future contemplated act is an act he can in good conscience perform? The judgment he will be making is an important one, and therefore it should follow upon sound and careful reasoning. There are four specific considerations that Theodosius will want to bring to mind: (1) the quality of his intention; (2) the nature of Act X itself; (3) the circumstances that are associated with the act; (4) the possible consequences of the act.

Intention. We can maintain our moral integrity in whatever we do only to the extent that we are guided by a good intention. We must always intend the good. We know that we need more than just a good intention (remember how the road to hell is paved), but we very definitely need at least that much. Someone can ruin an otherwise good act because he is moved to perform it by a bad intention. Lorenzo tells Luisa that she is the most virtuous woman he has ever met, a compliment which has a real basis in truth, but the purpose behind it is suspect, for Lorenzo is a real Lothario. Here we have an example of what T. S. Eliot described as "the final treason. Doing the right thing for the wrong reason." Lorenzo told the truth, but he did so in the attempt to open the way to achieving a less than edifying goal.

The nature of the act itself. Human acts can have intrinsic moral qualities, either positive or negative. If Theodosius correctly estimates Act X to be either intrinsically good or morally neutral, then, on that account, he has a green light to go ahead with it. But all must come to a definitive halt if he determines the act to be intrinsically evil. He could not, for example, do deliberate physical harm to an innocent person in order to bring about thereby some supposed good end. This would be to violate one of the most basic and venerable ethical precepts: evil is never deliberately to be done, even though we suppose good might come of it. We sometimes fool ourselves into thinking that we can succeed in bringing about a good end by evil means, but that never happens. In the short term, maybe, but not in the long term. I lie to Loraine with the purpose of making her feel good about herself—I really wanted Loraine to feel good about herself—but when she finds out about the lie she feels good neither about herself nor about me, and for good reason.

The circumstances associated with the act. No act is ever performed in a vacuum; it always takes place within a certain setting, a determinate situation with all that accompanies it: in a word, the circumstances of the act. These circumstances always have to be taken into account when we are evaluating any given act. Theodosius has the right intention for performing Act X, the act itself passes as being either intrinsically good or morally neutral, but upon further reflection he decides that the circumstances are not right, at least not at the moment.

At this point we will strip Act X of its anonymity. The act Theodosius is contemplating is withdrawing from his longtime business partnership with Ted Houston. On a recent Thursday afternoon he had made up his mind that, difficult though it would be, this was the right thing for him to do. He would inform Ted Houston of his decision the first thing the following Monday morning. But then, over that weekend, Ted Houston's father died suddenly of a heart attack. Because of this unfortunate turn of events, Theodosius revises his plans, decides that the circumstances are not right for informing Houston of the future dissolution of their partnership. He will wait for a more propitious time to act.

The possible consequences of the act. What might be its likely repercussions? This is one of the questions we should be asking ourselves when contemplating a future act. The answer to such a question can of course never be conclusive, for we are speculating about the future, about which nothing can be known with certainty. But not all speculations are equal, and some can carry more weight than others. Experience would be a key factor here, and those with more of it are usually more accurate in their conjectures about the future. We can have a reliable sense of the possible consequences of an act we are now contemplating if it is of a type we have performed often in the past, in circumstances comparable to those which we envision will accompany this performance of the act. If a pitcher knows that a certain batter he has often pitched against has a weakness for low inside fastballs, then whenever he faces that batter he will invariably be throwing low inside fastballs, confident that the consequences of his doing so will be favorable.

Ted Houston's devastated response to the death of his father led Theodosius to give more thorough thought to the possible consequences of his dissolving their business partnership. Ted Houston is a good man and a hard worker, but very high-strung. Theodosius recalled a couple of periods in the past when business was especially bad, and the disturbing way Houston had handled those situations. At times he seemed close to nervous collapse. Could Houston carry on without him? In the end, carefully weighing a number of factors, Theodosius decided that the possible consequences of dissolving the partnership—for the business, for Ted Houston personally, for Houston's family—could turn out to be quite negative, too negative in fact to justify his going ahead with his plan. The partnership would not be dissolved. He would stick with Ted Houston and make the best he could of a less than ideal situation.

The possible consequences of an act are what we would reasonably expect to follow were we to perform it, and we naturally take these into consideration as we contemplate the act. This would be *one* of the things we take into consideration, but it should not be the only thing. And we certainly would not want to make it the most important thing. There is, though, an ethical system which does precisely that. It gives primacy of place to consequences, and, appropriately enough, the name given to this system is consequentialism; it could also be called, less formally, bottom-line morality. It takes the position that the moral value of any act is to be determined chiefly, if not exclusively, by how things turn out as the result of performing the act. If the consequences are good, the act is good; if the consequences are bad, so too is the act that brought them about. The very simplicity of this way of distinguishing between right and wrong acts gives it a certain allure, but the reasoning that lies behind it is beset by a number of serious difficulties. I will limit myself to discussing but three of them.

First, consequentialism effectively denies the fact that there are human acts which are intrinsically evil, morally wrong in and of themselves. We call attention here to the pertinence of the rudimentary principle that it is never permissible to perform evil acts with the intention of achieving positive results through them. Besides, as noted above, and looking at it from a purely practical point of view, that approach simply does not work.

Whatever beneficial consequences we intend to bring about by an intrinsically evil act are inevitably vitiated by the evil act itself. The poison contained in the cause is communicated to the effect.

Second, while the possible consequences of an act, good in itself, might be judged to be sufficiently negative to demand that we refrain from performing the act, as happened in Theodosius's case discussed above, negative consequences need not always have that effect. Sometimes the act itself might be of such importance that it outweighs whatever negative consequences we can envision for it. Consider the case of Jasper, a junior member of a large corporation who knows for a fact that there are some serious illegal dealings going on in his department, with the tacit approval of a couple of powerful vice presidents. Jasper is an honest man, and he is thinking of blowing the whistle on the perpetrators of the illegalities. However, he knows that, should he do so, the consequences for himself would be far from pleasant. There would be a real possibility that he could lose his job. Nevertheless, Jasper decides to call attention to the illegal activity, having become convinced in conscience that it is the right thing to do, despite the possible dire consequences for himself. In a case like this, consequences become virtually irrelevant, in that they have no direct influence on the judgment of conscience which is being made.

Third, in making any judgment of conscience, it is very risky business putting all our eggs in the basket of consequences. We are conjecturing about the future, and therefore the consequences we are considering must necessarily be only *possible* consequences. We can never be sure of what will be the precise ramifications of any act we perform. And how often does it happen that we turn out to be flatly wrong, one way or another, in guessing what will happen as the consequential aftermath of our actions,? The rosy result I had optimistically anticipated for Act X turned out to be an unmitigated disaster, while, on the other hand, the baleful effects I felt sure would be produced by Act Y were never realized. And thus life keeps us on our toes with its surprises, big or little.

Forty-Two

The Intrinsic Worth of Human Acts

We saw that one of the things the conscientious Theodosius had to pay attention to when he was making a judgment of conscience about a future act he was contemplating was the nature of the act itself. Some human acts, taken just in themselves, considered in isolation from any context, are morally neutral. I lift my arm to scratch my head just above my right ear. Is that act morally right or morally wrong? We would all readily recognize that to be a silly question. There are any number of acts we perform over the course of a day—I would guess most of them on most days—routinized acts in the service of prosaic practicalities, which, just in themselves, bear no morally significant meaning.

Theodosius, clear and careful ethical thinker that he is, would stop giving any further consideration to a future act he was contemplating if he were to determine that the act itself was intrinsically evil, a bad act, in and of itself. To that type of act, and the morally neutral act, we add the intrinsically good act, to complete the picture. What is it about the intrinsically good and the intrinsically bad acts which allows us without hesitation to assign a clear moral value to their performance? We begin by reminding ourselves of some elementary principles. No act performed by us is subject to any moral evaluation at all unless it is a *human* act, which is to say, a voluntary act, that is, an act performed by someone who knows what he is doing and wills what he is doing. We are not automatons or robots, but free agents. An intrinsically evil act, then, is the kind of act which, if we are aware of what we are doing while we are doing it, and will what we are doing, we thereby unavoidably do evil. Adverting to an example cited earlier, deliberately, wantonly, and with malice of forethought to do grievous physical harm to an innocent human being is an intrinsically evil act. It would be impossible to perform such an act with a good intention; no set of circumstances could render it innocuous;

it could not become a permissible act by projecting putative beneficial consequences for it.

We consider the case of Leander, a man who has to rely on an array of medications because of various ailments with which he is burdened. His doctors are continuously challenged in their efforts to minimize and control the adverse side effects of these medications, but for all their care on occasion things go seriously wrong, and Leander can behave quite irrationally. So it happened one day when he was out at the local mall; suddenly he had a seizure, and for a brief period he lost control of himself, attacking a fellow shopper, an innocent passerby, beating him severely with his cane and causing appreciable physical injuries.

Looking at the incident from a purely objective point of view, we could say that Leander performed an intrinsically evil act; it was, taken in itself, simply a bad thing to do. However, because Leander, given the psychological state he was in at the time, lacked the requisite knowledge of the nature of the act, and thus could not will it for what it was, he could not be held to be *morally* responsible for what he did. He could not be considered to be guilty of the act, from a moral point of view.

A fuller understanding of the nature of intrinsically good and intrinsically evil acts can be had by reflecting on alternative names that are given to them—"inherently ordered acts" and "inherently disordered acts." The ideal ethical world is perfectly ordered, one in which reason reigns supreme; it is a blessedly peaceful world. We do not, unfortunately, live in a perfectly ordered world, and we would be naively optimistic to suppose that we ever will, but there is much to commend in giving due honor to an ideal, and keeping it before our mind's eye as something which, though perhaps never completely realizable, we should nonetheless be ever striving to realize insofar as we can. We may not be able ever to attain a perfectly ordered world, but an increasingly more ordered one is always feasible. Fostering such an attitude composes a very large part of what it means to be ethical. An inherently ordered act is one which fits into, which contributes to, the overall order which is the hallmark of the ideal ethical world, whereas the inherently disordered act, as its name suggests, detracts from that order and militates against it.

Another way of considering intrinsically good and intrinsically evil acts is under the rubric of their being either humanizing or dehumanizing acts. If, as I indicated at the beginning of this book, being ethical is essentially a matter of being human, in the full and unqualified sense—is, in other words, a matter of our measuring up to all we can be as rational creatures, on the natural level and even beyond the natural level—then the kinds of acts which we would want to be totally committed to performing would be humanizing acts (intrinsically good acts), and the kinds of acts to which we would want to be just as totally committed to avoiding would be dehumanizing acts (intrinsically evil acts).

The Golden Rule tells us that we should do unto others as we would want them to do unto us. Stated negatively: Don't behave towards others in ways you would not want them to behave towards you. We could not ask for a more lucid moral dictum, but there is a way of interpreting the Golden Rule, or rather of misinterpreting it, which effectively negates the notion that any act has intrinsic value attached to it, good or bad. According to this erroneous way of interpreting the dictum, an act is "good" only because of the positive results it will have for me if I perform it. In other words, so I suppose, people will respond to my act, in their own actions, in ways that will benefit me. The same with so-called "bad" acts; I call them bad because my performing them will result in people behaving toward me in ways that will not be to my benefit. So, the worth of an act is not intrinsic to it, but determined entirely by the kinds of responses, positive or negative, it draws from others. You doubtless see that what we have in this self-serving interpretation is an expression of consequentialism.

A human act is said to have intrinsic worth because we do not have to go beyond the act itself in order to determine its moral quality, either positive or negative. An intrinsically good act is such that, if things are in proper order with regard to intention, circumstances, and consequences, we cannot but act well in performing it. An intrinsically evil act is the type of act for the performance of which no adequate excuse can ever be offered; it is the type of act that one simply must not perform. An intrinsically evil act is dehumanizing and, among other things, such acts have the effect of a two-edged sword. They definitely wound the person who is the object of the act, but they wound the perpetrator of the act as well. And the wound suffered by the latter is much more grievous and lasting than that suffered by the former. Socrates was not speaking idly when he insisted that it is a greater evil to do injustice than to be the victim of injustice. The just who suffer injustice remain just, but those who do injustice become unjust.

Forty-Three
More on Circumstances

The circumstances associated with any act we perform can affect, positively or negatively, the moral quality of the act itself. Our word "circumstances" comes from two Latin ones, *circum stare*, "to stand around." The suggested imagery is vivid. Circumstances are what surround an act, give it a context, a definite location and coloration, and—this is what especially interests us—circumstances have the capacity to influence an act in such a way as to prompt us to alter our moral evaluation of it. An act that might be appropriate for one time and place could be quite inappropriate for another time and place. We would not consider it untoward for Simon to snuggle up to and engage in amorous antics with Sheila, his devoted and duly-wedded wife, in, say, the privacy of their den. However, were they to engage in such activity during a plenary meeting of the city council, of which both of them are members, their behavior would be rightly regarded as entirely out of place.

The circumstances associated with an act we are attempting to evaluate morally can affect that evaluation, then, but only within rather strict limitations. What we have identified as an intrinsically evil act—an inherently disordered act—cannot be miraculously transmogrified into a good act by circumstances. A tiger is a striped beast in the jungle; he retains his stripes should he subsequently find himself a resident of the Omaha Zoo. The ever perspicacious Aristotle once sagely observed that it is not possible to commit adultery with the right woman at the right time in the right circumstances, his point being that it is of the very nature of adultery that it is wrong under any conceivable circumstances. Adultery is an inherently disordered act because it directly attacks one of the foundational constituents of the social order, the institution of marriage. The man who cheats on his wife, or the woman who cheats on her husband, commits an offense against justice, their respective spouses being the offended parties.

A bad act cannot be made good by circumstances, but it can be made even worse by them. A man who engages in an adulterous affair does something bad, but he does something even worse if he initiates the affair while his wife is hundreds of miles away in California, attending the funeral of her parents, both of whom met sudden death in a car crash.

Circumstances have the most telling affect on those acts which, taken in themselves, can be judged to be either intrinsically good or morally neutral, for it can render such acts, given the circumstances in which they are performed, either morally dubious or downright morally bad. Such would be the bedroom behavior of Simon and Sheila if they were to engage in it in the public forum.

Consider another example. It could be altogether appropriate for a master plumber to give one of his apprentices a serious dressing down for some very sloppy work he had done. The preferable way for the master plumber to do this would be to take the apprentice aside and have an earnest one-on-one talk with him in private. Those would be the optimal circumstances for the admonishing act. But our master plumber chooses to give his apprentice his upbraiding in the presence of his fellow apprentices, and he overdoes it, subjecting the apprentice to a good deal of gratuitous verbal abuse. These circumstances appreciably diminish the moral rectitude of the master plumber's act. Moreover, and looking at it from a purely practical point of view, they very probably reduce, if not completely negate, the effectiveness of the admonitions delivered. Few of us appreciate being made to look like fools before an audience, although we might be prepared freely to admit to our foolish behavior in a non-threatening private setting.

In many if not in most cases, circumstances simply are what they are and we have no choice but to take them as they come and adjust to them accordingly. In such cases, if we judge that the circumstances would vitiate an act that otherwise could be considered as either inherently good or morally neutral, then we must stop and reconsider. When Justin first espies the pulchritudinous Felicia Fairfax across the crowded room on that enchanted early June evening, he immediately and helplessly falls in love with her and, right on the spot, he vows he is going to make her his bride, proposing to her at the earliest opportunity. A little later, while chatting at the punch bowl with a friend, he learns that the full title of his lady love is *Mrs.* Felicia Fairfax. Justin, heartbroken, remains close to the punch bowl for the remainder of the evening, vainly attempting to drown his sorrow in a liquid refreshment which, despite its name, lacks the kind of punch he felt he needs. But, crushed though he is, Justin is a man of honor, and makes a new vow: henceforth he will admire Mrs. Fairfax only from afar. She will become his Beatrice.

There are times when circumstances are not entirely propitious for the performance of a particular act, in that it will very likely generate some negative effects. But the act is such that it will brook no delay; it must be done, despite those effects. A supervisor may think it necessary to correct a subordinate in public, and perhaps rather harshly, even though he is aware that this will wound the sensitivities of the subordinate. He does this because the activity in which the subordinate is engaging is not only wrong-headed but dangerous to himself and others, and therefore requires an immediate response on his part. The situation was somewhat like that when Hop Hopkins, the seasoned hunter, yelled at his nephew: "Willie, when you carry that rifle you *always* keep the barrel pointing toward the ground, you *never* have it pointed at other people!"

Although we can seldom change circumstances, there are times when an act we are contemplating is not so compellingly urgent that its performance cannot be postponed, with no serious disadvantage, should present circumstances be not the best for its most effective performance. We can wait for better circumstances to come along.

Let us alter the little scenario sketched above, starring Justin and Felicia Fairfax. Justin, standing by the punch bowl, discovers, to his unparalleled delight, that his inamorata is blessedly single, and with no known serious suitor in sight. His initial impulse, after learning this news, is to gulp down his cup of punch and dash across the crowded room, drop dramatically to his knees in front of Felicia, and propose marriage to her then and there, after of course first introducing himself. But Justin, for all his sometimes intemperate impetuosity, thinks better of this approach, and decides that he will bide his time, waiting for more appropriate circumstances for the proposal.

In everything said here so far we have been concentrating on how circumstances affect an act which they surround. But influence can be exerted in the opposite direction as well. An act can affect circumstances, for better or for worse. A significant plateau in ethical thinking has been reached when we begin to realize that circumstances, forbiddingly immutable though they may sometime appear, are subject to change, for the better, by actions, our actions. We may not be able, by our actions, to change *the* world, but there are other smaller worlds which we inhabit, quite familiar to us, which are open to significant alteration by how we behave in those worlds.

Forty-Four

More on Intention

There is no need to belabor the point, already made with sufficient emphasis, that while a good intention is a necessary condition for a sound moral act, it cannot alone determine the righteousness of the act. To be sure, I must always intend, in all of my actions, the good, but I must do more than just that.

Intention, in ethics, refers to the objects toward which our actions are directed. To intend something is to fix one's sights on a particular end, perceived as a good, and therefore as something which one desires to attain. For the desire to be fulfilled by the attainment of a particular end, if it is to have sufficient efficacy, it must be coupled with a willingness on the part of the desiring subject to adopt the means that are necessary to attain the end. In short, I can be said to be seriously intending something if (a) I identify it as a desirable good, and (b) I am willing to do whatever needs to be done to attain it.

For an act to be morally sound, it must have a good intention behind it. That much is clear, but what is the difference between a good intention and a bad intention? You will recall the distinction between a real good (one that will in fact be perfective of us as persons) and an apparent good (one that will *not* be perfective of us as persons). The implication of that distinction is that while we always choose what we perceive will be good for us, our perceptions in this critical matter are sometimes not as reliable as we would want them to be, and we end up pursuing apparent goods instead of real ones. We chase after things that will damage us rather than benefit us.

But because we are psychologically constituted in such a way that we pursue only what we perceive to be good, whether or not it is in fact good, then, from a *subjective* point of view—that is, from the point of view of the acting person—we are always intending the good. This is only to say that we always pursue and seek to possess what we perceive to be good, even though, in any particular case, our perceptions may be wrong. In such a case, i.e., where I am pursuing an apparent good rather than a real one, my intention, though objectively speaking a bad one (because it will not procure for me what is truly perfective of myself as a person) is nonetheless taken by me to be a good intention. The situation really couldn't be otherwise, for our intentions cannot be separated from the objects toward which they are directed, and because I perceive something as good, even though mistakenly, I intend it as good.

To sum up: A good intention, objectively considered, is one which is directed toward an objectively good end. A bad intention is one which is directed toward an objectively bad end.

We can spoil an otherwise good act by having as the motivating factor behind it an objectively bad intention. What is happening in such a case would be an instance of our "doing the right thing for the wrong reason." A standard example of this, a favorite of the ethics textbooks, is the man who gives money to the poor only to enhance his reputation as a magnanimous philanthropist. Such a man is Halifax, who is regularly contributing large sums to the indigent, while at the same time taking care that his contributions receive maximum coverage by the local media. The sad fact of the matter is that Halifax harbors little genuine concern for the poor. On the other hand, he is much concerned with his public image. Objectively speaking, Halifax's philanthropy is motivated by a bad intention. Ideally, he should be aiding the poor because that is an intrinsically good thing to do. But it is the enhancement of his reputation that is the intention that drives his actions (which has much to do with the idea he has of one day running for governor), and although that is for him an apparent good rather than a real one, he would be incapable of pursuing it if he did not intend it as a good.

Does the money that Halifax regularly gives to the poor actually benefit the poor, despite the objectively bad intention behind his actions? There is no reason why it should not. But that does not make Halifax a truly generous man. It is not the virtue of generosity that governs his actions.

A good intention cannot transform a bad act into a good one. When we think otherwise we succumb to that classical fallacy which supposes that a good end can be achieved by evil means. Consider the case of Mr. Hood, who is every bit as generous as Halifax in giving money to the poor, and with the purest of intentions. Unlike Halifax, he has the highest regard for the poor, loves them dearly, and has their welfare always uppermost in mind. But Mr. Hood gets the ample funds he donates to the poor by printing thousands upon thousands of dollars in counterfeit bills, in the art of doing which he has become a past master. Because he seeks to achieve a good end through evil means, the end is thus contaminated, and, as it turns out, quite ironically, Mr. Hood is no more a truly generous man than is Halifax. There is no virtue in being generous through criminal activity.

An intention, good or bad, can give distinct moral coloration to what would otherwise be a morally neutral act. Scratching one's head above the right ear is a morally insignificant act, taken in itself, but what if that act is the decided-upon signal that a terrorist gives to his comrade in crime to tell him to detonate a bomb that, exploding in a crowded market place, will cause the death of dozens of innocent people? In that situation, scratching one's head ceases to be a morally neutral act and becomes an evil one.

The critical importance of intention for ethics is dramatically demonstrated by the weight attached to it by civil law. Max can be sentenced to prison for a lengthy period of time if it can be proved in a court of law that he intended to murder Maureen, although he never so much as laid a violent finger on the woman. The intent to murder is a punishable crime, even though the intention is never actually realized.

We can form an intention, good or bad, and never follow through on it. If the intention is good, this can make for an awkward state of affairs. It can be a bit painful to reflect on all those nice little things we planned to do, not to speak of all the large and noble things, that, somehow, we never got around to doing. A good act must be preceded by a good intention, but the act will never follow unless we make good on the intention. As to failing to follow through on a bad intention, that does not necessarily dissipate guilt. If I intend to do positive evil to another person, but then do not follow through on my intention, the person targeted by me may be unscathed, but I have nonetheless done moral damage to myself. The man who seriously intends to murder, even though he does not in fact murder, harbors a murderous heart.

Forty-Five

Does the Individual Person Have the Final Say?

The importance of the subjective dimension of moral reasoning is not to be minimized, for, after all, the center and source of moral reasoning is none other than the human subject, the person. It is up to each individual, as a moral agent, to shape and direct his behavior by making the pivotal distinction between moral right and wrong. Such is the case with Waldo, such is the case with every adult human being. When it comes to making moral judgments concerning his own person and behavior, Waldo and Waldo alone must act as judge. This is the principal responsibility we have as moral agents, and we cannot pass it on to anyone else. In this sense each of us, as judges, can be said to have the final say in moral matters, pretty much the same way as a civil judge has the final say in matters pertaining to civil law.

A civil judge has the final say in legal matters, as one whose responsibility it is to adjudicate, to interpret the law, to specify how it is to be applied in particular cases. But a judge does not make laws; that is the function of the legislature. The same holds true in the moral realm, where each of us acts as a judge. In the moral realm we make our judgments according to the law, but, like the civil judge, we do not make the laws according to which we make our judgments. The law that governs the moral realm is, in its comprehensive form, the natural law, that law that governs all human reasoning as it pertains to morality.

This point of view would be contested by the individualist, who believes himself to be not only a judge in moral matters, but a legislator as well. It is he, so he believes, who in any given instance is to determine what is morally right and wrong. He is the one who sets the standards. Just how those standards are determined would vary greatly, depending on the personality of the individualist himself. One individualist might give a great deal of careful thought to the matter, and map out a rather elaborate moral

code to which he gives loyal, perhaps unqualified, obeisance. Another individualist may proceed on a purely *ad hoc* basis, making up the rules as he
goes along, to match the demands of his appetites. For the latter type, what
is right or wrong in any particular instance may be decided by what emotion dictates, or whim.

What is common to all individualists is that they consider themselves
to be legislators of morality. They would be unanimous in repudiating the
idea of natural law. For them, there are no moral principles which are common to all. The purest, and most incoherent, form of individualism main-
tains that morality is specific to each individual. Moral standards are set by
each individual, and apply only to the individual who sets them. Morality
thus becomes purely private.

There is a bit of the individualist in all of us. There are times when we
are seized by a selfish, myopic urge to insist on doing things our way, no
matter what, which blinds us to the obvious fact that our way is not always
the best way. There is something perversely seductive in the idea of playing
in a game where you make up the rules, and change them continuously as
self-serving exigencies demand, but that kind of solitaire quickly loses its
tang. We are, in spite of ourselves, social animals.

No attempt to apply the individualistic view of morality on a large scale
could ever be successful, for it would result in utter social chaos. Imagine
what would happen to any civil society if it had no legislative body, and it
was left to each individual to govern himself as he saw fit, "looking after
Number One" being his guiding moral principle. The citizens of that un-
happy society would find themselves back in Thomas Hobbes's state of nature, where life is solitary, poor, nasty, brutish, and short.

We can no more make up the rules in morals than we can in mathematics. Though it is not always easy to say why it is so, mathematics reflects
the way the world actually is in its quantitative manifestations. The mathematician does not make up the rules, he discovers them, and he thus learns
something, albeit perhaps only obliquely, about how the world we live in
works. We are not all mathematicians, but we are all moralists, and when
we think clearly and correctly about moral matters we discover something
about how the moral world is ordered. We become ethical realists.

But what are we to say about the idea of a purely private morality,
which some individualists are wont to advocate? There is no such thing. A

"purely private morality" is a contradiction in terms, and makes as much sense as a "purely private language." Morality is a communal reality, as is language. The purpose of language is not to talk to oneself but to communicate with others, and to fulfill that purpose a language must be the shared property of many. So too with morality. Its purpose is to govern behavior *among* people, and it can only do this if its basic principles are shared by all the people whose behavior it directly concerns.

Forty-Six

Is It All Relative?

Is there relativism in ethics? Yes, of course, and necessarily so. Case in point: the basic principles of ethical behavior cannot be applied mechanically, in precisely the same way in each and every case. Those principles must be applied relatively, that is to say, by taking into account the particulars that pertain to the individual cases. We have seen how important it is to consider the circumstances in which a particular act is embedded so as to arrive at a complete reading of the moral quality of the act. There must be consonance between act and circumstances. Everyone is obliged to live a temperate life, but a temperate life does not mean the same thing for everyone. What would be temperate behavior for the married man would not be so for a Benedictine monk. Both must live temperately, but they live temperately in different ways, relative to their different states in life.

To acknowledge the necessary role of relativism in ethics is by no means to subscribe to a philosophical point of view called moral relativism. Here we have something altogether different. The individualism previously discussed would be an example of an extreme form of moral relativism. At the heart of moral relativism is the rejection of the notion of universal moral principles—moral principles applicable to all human beings. Accordingly, moral relativism would have no patience with the idea of moral absolutes, for a moral absolute is simply an ethical principle which has universal application. When not rejecting them peremptorily, the relativist will sometimes attempt to show that moral absolutes, despite the claims made for them, are really relative.

We need to address directly this matter of moral absolutes. There seems to be a noticeable number of people today who are made positively nervous by the very idea of absolutes, moral or otherwise. There is nothing to be nervous about, as a little systematic reflection will show. To begin, some elementary clarifications are in order. We are in the habit of using the term "absolute" as a noun, as if referring to an entity of some sort, and that gets us off on the wrong foot. "Absolute" is in the first instance an adjective, a qualifier of a noun, as in the phrase "absolute zero." For our concerns, the noun which this controversial adjective is called upon to qualify is "statement." Most people who deny absolutes are really denying absolute statements; more particularly, they are denying that any statement can be absolutely true. Someone who would deny a place on the planet for absolutely true statements could be called an epistemological relativist.

It is of the very nature of any statement that it must be either true or false. The relativist contends that any purportedly true statement is only relatively true, but in this the relativist is committing himself to a complete fiction. There is no such thing as a relatively true statement. Every true statement, if it is in fact true, is absolutely true. It could not be anything but. What is an absolutely true statement? It is simply one that admits of no exceptions. Are there absolutely false statements? Yes. An absolutely false statement would be one which, if true, would be in conflict with reality. "Ulysses S. Grant was the twelfth president of the United States" is an absolutely false statement, for, if it were true, it would be at odds with the incontestable facts of history.

The distinction between truth and falsity in statements reflects the deeper ontological distinction between "is" and "is not," between being and non-being. If Portia is in Portland, she is not in Pocatello. Let us say that Portia is, as matter of fact, in Portland. Then the statement, "Portia is in Portland," is absolutely true, and the statement, "Portia is not in Portland" is absolutely false.

If one were to maintain that a purportedly true statement does in fact admit of exceptions, that would mean that it could be true and false at one and the same time, and if we are willing to concede that, we are caught up in contradiction. The mathematical statement, $2 + 2 = 4$, is absolutely true. Can you think of an exception to it? That plain arithmetical truth is but one of myriads of absolute truths in which we are fairly swimming, and without which we could not make sense of the world in which we live.

But the tough question we have to face has to do with moral statements. Are there moral absolutes, which is to say, are there statements having to do with moral matters which can be regarded as absolutely true, i.e., admitting of no exceptions? Most of us would have little trouble in acknowledging 2 + 2 = 4 to be absolutely true, but how about statements such as the following: "It is always right to come to the aid of those in perilous need." "It is never right to do wanton harm to others." "It is never right to distort the truth in communicating with those who have a right to know." "It is always right to take proper care of one's health so as to be able to meet the obligations of one's state in life." "It is always right to respect and defend the good name of others." "It is never right to appropriate the property of others without their knowledge and permission."

Those are all very general moral principles, and we are fully justified in recognizing them as absolutely true. For short, we could call them moral absolutes. Because they are true as general principles, any more particular principles correctly derived as corollaries of them could also deserve to be designated moral absolutes. A moral absolute is simply a statement pertaining to moral matters that admits of no exceptions. The test of a moral absolute, then, is couched in that pregnant phrase, "admits of no exceptions." Anyone who would want to deny absolute status to any of the general moral principles listed above must be prepared to state what he would regard as permissible exceptions to them, and then give arguments for his position.

Individualists, as I mentioned, represent the extreme position of moral relativism, but not all moral relativists are individualists. There is a more mild form of moral relativism which does not deny that there are certain moral principles which are very general in nature, held in common by large numbers of people representing particular cultures, or representing particular ethnic, national, or religious groups, but would nonetheless insist that there are no truly universal moral principles, that is, principles applying to mankind as such and irrespective of cultural, ethnic, or national differences. These mild moral relativists would call attention to the fact, easily checked by a comparison of almost any two cultures, that there are discrepancies to be noted, sometimes significant ones, in what people regard as morally right and wrong.

And then there is the chronological factor to consider. In any particular culture, such as our own, ideas regarding moral right and wrong would seem to change over time. Americans of the early twenty-first century find morally acceptable certain types of behavior that Americans of the mid-nineteenth century, by and large, would have regarded as positively abhorrent. Is this not a good argument for moral relativism? Does it not force us to abandon the idea that there are in fact universal moral universals, principles that apply to all people of all times?

There has been much rushing to judgment on this question, resulting from a decidedly selective way of looking at the data. We have allowed ourselves to become so mesmerized by the undeniable relativistic aspects of human morality that we often fail to notice the non-relativistic substructure which underpins them. We have become so enchanted by the peripheral ways in which people are morally different that we miss the essential ways in which they are morally the same. As a result, we have a schooled tendency to look right by, as if they did not even exist, the universal moral principles, the moral absolutes, which are collectively summed up in what we call the natural law.

All peoples in all places and at all times have acknowledged that life is precious and is to be preserved and protected, that spouses are to be faithful to one another, that children are to be cherished and properly educated, that it is right to be loyal and wrong to betray, that truth is one of the greatest of goods and deception is baneful, that cooperation is preferable to dissension, amity to animosity, that the goods of the earth are to be carefully conserved. Men have and do differ over particulars, but there has been a pervasive, enduring pattern of basic agreement, spanning the full course of human history, regarding general principles, the foundational moral truths that bind us together as a race.

But Rollie the Relativist wants to have the last word here. You have the floor, Rollie, please proceed. Let us dialogue.

"I don't believe a bit of it. There are no moral absolutes. It's all relative."

"All? I think you mean to say, everything pertaining to morality."

"I mean to say what I said. Everything is relative, period."

"You believe, then, that there are no statements that can be held to be absolutely true?"

"That is what I believe."

"What about that statement?"

"What statement?"

"There are no statements that can be held to be absolutely true?"

"Rollie?"

"Rollie?"

Forty-Seven

A Case in Point

On December 10, 1948, the General Assembly of the United Nations published a memorable document called the Universal Declaration of Human Rights. The Preamble of the document described it as "a common standard of achievement for all peoples and all nations," made reference to "all members of the human family," spoke of "the dignity and worth of the human person," and gave special emphasis to "the conscience of mankind." Article 1 declares that, "All human beings . . . are endowed with reason and conscience and should act toward one another in a spirit of brotherhood." Among the various rights the document specifies as belonging to all human beings is "the right to life, liberty, and security of person" (Article 3), and "the right to recognition everywhere as a person" (Article 6). The language used throughout the document expresses clearly, emphatically even, the conviction on the part of its framers that there are universal principles of morality which are meant to govern and guide the behavior of the whole of humankind. The document stands as an explicit and dramatic attestation of the existence of the natural law. It could not have been written without that law.

The Universal Declaration of Human Rights was drawn up and agreed to by what was very probably the most diverse collection of human beings which had ever been gathered together in one place. They represented a microcosm of the race itself. It has now been sixty years since the publication of the document, and although one can wonder just what real practical effect it has had on the world to which it was addressed, it is hard to imagine that the document, in its main outlines, could ever be explicitly repudiated.

The whole tone of the document makes clear the proper way in which a reader is to understand the various specific "declarations" it is making— as formal statements of moral matters of fact. The document is not *establishing* rights, is not decreeing them into existence as it were, but simply calling attention to and demanding proper recognition of what are taken to be objective realities which are already firmly and permanently in place. The document is implicitly recognizing the existence of an objective moral order, a moral order which man does not invent but to which he is subject. Especially interesting, I think, is the Declaration's allusion to "the conscience of mankind." Can not that be understood as referring to a shared moral consciousness, by which we distinguish between moral right and wrong and acknowledge general ethical principles which are applicable to the entire race? The Declaration is telling us that, on the most basic level, when we think about moral matters, we think alike.

At this point, an objection to the position I am advancing here might be lodged, expressed in the following terms: "I agree that there are certain very basic moral tenets that seem to be shared by all human beings, and I suppose that supports the contention that we are to be considered a single race. But you seem to be suggesting that those principles enjoy some sort of objective status, that they rank as 'givens' of nature. I don't agree with that. Those universal moral principles, such as they are, have their source in the human mind itself, are, to be more scientific about it, the inventions of natural selection, and thus doubtless have something to do with our survival as a species."

If to the protestor I only "seem to be suggesting" that universal moral principles "enjoy some sort of objective status," then I have been insufficiently clear in my language. I am not merely suggesting, but explicitly arguing, that there is an objective moral order which, I would further contend, is roughly analogous to the objective physical order. Therefore, just as there are physical laws that govern all that is made of matter, so there are moral laws that enlighten, guide, and give guiding impetus to that peculiar and often exasperatingly erratic moral agent we call a human person. The physical laws really exist, and without hesitation we recognize that they are the discoveries, not the inventions, of the human intellect. The laws of morality also really exist, and demand our obedience, though in an obviously different but nonetheless significantly comparable way: the physical laws coerce our obedience, whereas the moral laws are obeyed freely. Both are seen by us to have their origins in a source that transcends the purely human.

Though the principles of the natural law are not the inventions of the human intellect, they are discovered through the exercise of the human intellect; they reveal themselves as the result of our studied considerations of all aspects of human behavior as related to the realm of morality. More concretely, it is through the reflective thought we give to our interpersonal dealings with one another, and with our involvements with the world at large, that we discover the principles of the natural law. This is not radically different from the way the human intellect discovers the laws that govern the physical universe. As with the physical laws, so too with the moral laws, we come to have explicit knowledge of them through the active engagement of the human intellect with objective reality.

The nature of the natural law is such, then, that its principles are discovered within ourselves, but, note well, as the result of our conscious, rational engagement with that which is external to ourselves, principally with the social milieu constituted by the human community. The human intellect is so framed that it has the innate capacity, through the exercise of its reasoning powers, to discover, at the most elementary level, the crucial distinction between moral right and wrong, and to realize that the distinction has objective standing.

A suggestive comparison: professional linguists have argued that human beings have an innate capacity to learn language, to which they have given the name Universal Grammar. I would argue that there is something analogous to that in the moral realm. All human beings, by dint of the fact that they are rational creatures, have a built-in capacity to discover the basic principles of morality. This can be said to be proved by the remarkable fact that we all speak essentially the same moral language, a language that has its roots in the natural law.

As to the attempt to give a Darwinian twist to universal moral principles, what, one might ask, is the survival value of, "It is better to suffer injustice than to perpetrate it," or, "Greater love than this no one has, that one lay down his life for his friends"? The efforts which have been made to force a fit between altruistic behavior and the Procrustean Bed of natural selection have produced singularly unconvincing results. But perhaps it could be argued, after all, that there is a certain survival value relating to Socrates' dictum regarding the preferability of suffering injustice over perpetrating it: enduring that kind of suffering may be said to ensure our survival precisely as rational creatures. And the same may be said of laying down one's life for one's friends. Human acts of that exceptional kind would be the preservatives of our humanity.

The British mathematician G. H. Hardy wrote the following: "I believe that mathematical reality lies outside us, that our function is to discover or *observe* it, and that the theorems which we prove, and which we describe grandiloquently as our "creations," are simply our notes to our observations." (*A Mathematician's Apology*, 2005, pp. 123–24.) Later in the same book he wrote: "Pure mathematics, on the other hand, seems to me a rock on which all idealism founders: 317 is a prime, not because we think so, or because our minds are shaped in one way rather than in another, but *because it is so*, because mathematical reality is built that way." (Ibid., p. 130.) We can speak with the same kind of assurance about the moral realm. We are able to identify an objectively founded distinction between right and wrong because it is a real distinction, reflecting the way the moral world is built.

Forty Eight
The Last Word

"Become what you are." So wrote the ancient Greek poet Pindar. What was he driving at? He was inviting people, urging them, to live up to their proper nature, to become fully human. Being fully human is just another way of expressing the subject with which this book has been concerne—being ethical. To be ethical, to live an ethical life, a virtuous life, simply means to live up to our proper natures as rational creatures. That is a point we have made much of throughout the course of the book, and, given its importance, it is worth repeating at book's end. An ethical person, a morally good person, is an eminently rational person.

In citing the first principle of ethical thought—that good is to be done and evil avoided— we focused our attention on the commanding role that the good plays in our lives. It is the foundational motivating factor for everything we do. We always go after what we perceive to be good; we cannot do otherwise. The work of artists is ordered toward producing something beautiful which is separate from themselves, a luminous artifact. For those who are intent upon pursuing the moral good, the work of art they seek to bring to perfection is themselves, their very persons, and every good they gain contributes to the special kind of creativity to which they are dedicated. Eventually the distinction between pursuer and pursued blurs, then coalesces; the good they aspire after is in its essence the good they want to be.

Being ethical is a mode of existing, a way of life, is, in fact, life itself, lived to the fullest, and its principal occupation, pursuing the good, is life-long. The consistent pursuit of the good is exacting, and requires endurance, perseverance; that is where virtue comes in, giving us the strength to carry on boldly and with good humor the supremely important endeavor of becoming what we are meant to be. Happiness, we saw, is grounded in action, is in fact one and the same with the action which we call virtuous, because it is given to the pursuit of what is truly good.

To be ethical means to be fully human, yes, and more, for becoming fully human entails moving beyond the exclusively human. The peculiar mystery of the human condition, its principal paradox, is that we can only completely succeed in becoming what we are by transcending what we are, and this is so because of the insuperable limitations in what our humanness, taken in itself, is capable of offering us. The ethical life must needs be one of continual ascension. The good which by nature we cannot help but seek is, at bottom, more total and splendid than what by nature we are capable of conceiving, and very much more than what we are capable of imagining. It is nothing else but *the* Good, the absolute and unqualified Good, ever inviting, ever beckoning us on.